FIXED (

by Kerry Underwood

© Kerry Underwood 2004

Published by
xpl publishing
195 Berkhamstead Road
Chesham
Bucks
HP5 3AP

ISBN 1 85811 323 7

All rights reserved. No part of this publication may be reproduced, stored in a retrieval system, or transmitted, in any form or by any means, electronic, mechanical, photocopying, recording or otherwise, without the prior permission of the publisher.

The moral right of the author has been asserted.

Typeset by Jane Conway

Cover design by Jane Conway
Cover photography by Jon Adams

Printed in Great Britain by Lightning Source

Dedication

To my niece

Marie

Thanks to

Claire Beaumont

Andrew Griffin

Aye Limbin

Robert Males

Claire McParland

Sandra Place

Alan Rimmer

CONTENTS

TABLE OF CASES

Cases Referred To

Cases Considered

Aiden Shipping Ltd. v Interbulk Ltd. [1986] AC 965, House of Lords

Callery v Gray [2001] 1 WLR 2112, Court of Appeal, [2001] 2 Costs LR 163,
    Court of Appeal
Callery v Gray (No. 2) [2001] 1 WLR 2142, Court of Appeal, [2001] 2 Costs LR,
    205, Court of Appeal

Re Eastwood [1980] 1 WLR 396

Finley v Glaxo Laboratories [1989] Costs Law Reports 106

Godwin v Swindon Borough Council [2002] 1 WLR 997

Halloran v Delaney [2002] 3 Costs LR 503, Court of Appeal
Hill v Bailey Times Law Reports, 5 January 2004, High Court
Hodgson v Imperial Tobacco [1998] 1 WLR, Court of Appeal
Hoffman La Roche v Secretary of State for Trade and Industry [1975] AC 295

Jemma Trust Company Ltd. V (1) Peter D'Arcy Liptrott (2) John Forrester (3)
    Kippax Beaumont Lewis [2003] EWCA Civ 1476 Unreported, 24 October 2003,
    Court of Appeal
Johnson v Reed Corrugated Cases Ltd. [1992] 1 AER 169

Kraaijfeld and Others v Gedeputeerde Staten van Zuid-Holland (Case C–72/95)
    [1997] Env. L.R. 265

Leopold Lazarus v Secretary of State for Trade and Industry [1976] Cost Law
    Reports, Core Volume 62
Loveday v Renton and Another (No. 2) [1992] 3 AER 184

Maltby v D.J. Freeman [1978] 1 WLR 431
McDonald v Horn [1995] ICR 685, Court of Appeal

New Zealand Maori Council v Attorney-General of New Zealand [1994] AC 466,
    Privy Council

Property and Reversionary Investment Corporation Ltd. v Secretary of State for
    the Environment [1975] 1 WLR 1504

R. v Inland Revenue Commissioners, ex parte National Federation of Self-
    Employed [1982] AC 617, House of Lords
R. v Wilkinson [1980] 1 WLR 396
Re C (Legal Aid: Preparation of Bill of Costs) [2001] 1 FLR 602

Treasury Solicitor v Regester [1978] 1 WLR 446

Wong v Vizards [1997] 2 Costs LR 46
Wraith v Sheffield Forgemasters Ltd. [1998] 1 WLR 132, Court of Appeal

INTRODUCTION

The introduction of fixed costs represents one of the greatest changes in funding in the history of English law.

It is as significant as the creation of legal aid and its subsequent abolition and much more significant than conditional fees.

Where fixed costs tread contingency fees will follow. We are now no more than five years away from a full-blown United States-style contingency fee scheme.

Although fixed costs only operate in a limited area at present – unissued road traffic accident cases valued at £10,000 or less and some Court of Protection work – they will spread quickly to other areas and the value of claims caught will increase. Employers' liability cases are likely to be next, followed by public liability cases and then clinical negligence cases. Unifying the fast-track and fixed fee schemes should be a matter of months not years.

Conditional fee success fees have now been fixed in *all* road traffic accident cases, whatever their value and whether issued or not and whether settled or not. Counsel's conditional fee success fees are also fixed.

Fixed costs represent an opportunity to rescue a civil justice system that, like most public services, is in terrible trouble. Alienation of the public from the courts is arguably as dangerous as alienation of the public from elections.

The facts speak for themselves. The Court of Appeal's Civil Division figures show that the number of appeals filed has dropped in each of the last four years and at 1,287 in 2001–02 was 21.86% lower than in 1997–8 when 1,647 appeals were lodged.*

Over the same period claims lodged in the High Court dropped a staggering 65.87% from 159,806 in 1997 to 54,543 in 2002.** Court Service figures for the County Courts show that the number of claims fell by 25% from 2 million to 1.5 million in the period 1997–2001.

The dwindling use of the civil courts and the resulting loss in court fees is a pressing issue for the Court Service and the Lord Chancellor's Department or whatever it is now called. The Supreme Court suffered a £55 million deficit in 2002 leading to a review of court fees designed to turn the civil courts into profit-making entities.

This has led to fears that, in the absence of legal aid, access to justice will be further denied to people because court fees will rise, fewer claims will be issued and court fees will rise and so on.

Of course it could be that Britain has become a less complaining, less litigious and more harmonious country over that time but somehow I do not think that that is the explanation.

Fixed costs will go a long way to reassuring the public that legal costs, while not cheap, can be predictable. This allows the individual to make an informed decision. The average lawyer's response to a query about how much a case will cost makes the plumber's intake of breath seem almost inaudible.

Fixed costs also allow other costs to be purged from the system. For example, in most fixed costs cases it will be unnecessary to take out after-the-event insurance, as the liability will be certain and relatively low.

---

*   Source: *The Lawyer*, 6 January 2003.
** Source: *The Lawyer*, 9 June 2003.

More importantly fixed costs will benefit the efficient firms who make use of modern technology and use systems to ensure that knowledge is held, shared and used rather than re-inventing the wheel on each and every file, and of course charging for it. Drive out the hourly rate and you drive out the dinosaurs, the dawdlers and the ditherers.

All lawyers have a duty to make fixed costs work. If they do not work then lawyers will lose their monopoly over court work, and once that happens most firms will go out of business.

It is as simple as that. Good luck.

Kerry Underwood
Bovingdon
Hertfordshire
April 2004

CHAPTER 1
WHAT IS COVERED?

CHAPTER 1
WHAT IS COVERED?

Part 45.7(2) of the Civil Procedure Rules deals with what is covered by the fixed recoverable costs scheme:

> (2) This Section applies where –
>
>   (a) the dispute arises from a road traffic accident;
>
>   (b) the agreed damages include damages in respect of personal injury, damage to property, or both;
>
>   (c) the total value of the agreed damages does not exceed £10,000; and
>
>   (d) if a claim had been issued for the amount of the agreed damages, the small claims track would not have been the normal track for that claim.

In the Practice Direction relating to Part 45, under the heading "Scope" Section 25A reads as follows:

> 25A.1 Section II of Part 45 ("the Section") provides for certain fixed costs to be recoverable between the parties in respect of costs incurred in disputes which are settled prior to proceedings being issued. This Section applies to road traffic accident disputes as defined in rule 45.7(4)(a), where the accident which gave rise to the dispute occurred on or after 6 October 2003.

25A.2   The Section does not apply to disputes where the total agreed value of the damages is within the small claims limit or exceeds £10,000.

Rule 26.8(2) sets out how the financial value of a claim is assessed for the purposes of allocation to track.

25A.3   Fixed recoverable costs are to be calculated by reference to the amount of agreed damages which are payable to the receiving party. In calculating the amount of these damages –

(a) account must be taken of both general and special damages and interest;

(b) any interim payments made must be included;

(c) where the parties have agreed an element of contributory negligence, the amount of damages attributed to that negligence must be deducted.

(d) any amount required by statute to be paid by the compensating party directly to a third party (such as sums paid by way of compensation recovery payments and National Health Service expenses) must not be included.

25A.4   The Section applies to cases which fall within the scope of the Uninsured Drivers Agreement dated 13 August 1999. The Section does not apply to cases which fall within the scope of the Untraced Drivers Agreement dated 14 February 2003.

Small Claims

A claim which, had it been issued, would normally have been assigned to the small claims track is *not* covered by the scheme (45.7(2)(d)) and thus costs are not recoverable in small claims.

Note that the small claims limit is £1,000 in relation to personal injury but £5,000 otherwise. Thus either the damages for personal injury must exceed £1,000 or the *total* settlement must exceed £5,000.

Example

Damages for personal injury	750.00
Other damages (e.g. car)	4,000.00
	———
	4,750.00
	———

Neither threshold is crossed, thus this claim would have been assigned to the small claims track and fixed costs are *not* recoverable.

Example

Damages for personal injury	1,005.00
Other damages	245.00
	———
	1,250.00
	———

Personal injury threshold is crossed and thus this claim would *not* have been assigned to the small claims track and fixed costs *are* recoverable.

Example

Damages for personal injury	750.00
Other damages	4,300.00
	————
	5,050.00
	————

Overall threshold of £5,000 is crossed and thus this claim would *not* have been assigned to the small claims track and fixed costs *are* recoverable.

Any increase in the small claims track limit will have a very significant effect on fixed recoverable costs. However now that agreement has been reached on fixed costs and they have been introduced it is very unlikely that the small claims limit will be altered in the near future, (but see the proposals of the Department for Work and Pensions – Chapter 9 "The Future").

Rule 26.6 provides for when the small claims track is the normal track.

Road Traffic Accident

Fixed recoverable costs apply only where the dispute arises from a road traffic accident (45.7(2)(a)).

Part 45.7(4) states:

(4) In this Section –

(a) "road traffic accident" means an accident resulting in bodily injury to any person or damage to property caused by, or arising out of, the use of a motor vehicle on a road or other public place in England and Wales;

(b) "motor vehicle" means a mechanically propelled vehicle intended for use on roads; and

(c) "road" means any highway and any other road to which the public has access and includes bridges over which a road passes."

Jurisdiction

Only accidents occurring in the jurisdiction of England and Wales are covered (45.7(4)(a)). Thus accidents in Scotland or Northern Ireland, or any other jurisdiction, are not within the scheme.

Personal Injury

Unfortunately the Rule uses different terms in different parts leaving open the question of whether a claim for just nervous shock is covered.

Part 45.7(2)(b) refers to "damages in respect of personal injury" and a bracketed note under 45.7(3) states:

(Rule 2.3 defines "personal injuries" as including any disease and any impairment of a person's physical or mental condition.)

So far so good.

However to come within the scheme the dispute must arise from a "road traffic accident" (45.7(2)(a)).

As we have seen 45.7(4)(a) defines "road traffic accident" as meaning "an accident resulting in bodily injury to any person or damage ...."

Thus under this definition there must be *bodily* injury. The New Shorter Oxford English Dictionary defines bodily as

> "of, belonging to, or affecting the human body or physical nature".

Thus it does not cover pure psychiatric or mental injury.

Thus if there is no bodily, that is physical, injury to *anyone* then the matter is not covered by the fixed recoverable costs scheme, as Part 45.7(2)(a), read in conjunction with 45.7(4)(a), is not satisfied.

However if *any* person suffers physical injury in the accident then anyone else's claim, even if for just psychiatric injury, will be covered by the scheme.

Example

Dennis Driver is physically injured. Peter Passenger suffers nervous shock only. Peter Passenger's claim, as well as that of Dennis Driver, is covered by the scheme as "road traffic accident" means "an accident resulting in bodily injury to *any* person" (45.7(4)(a)) (my emphasis).

Litigants in Person

The scheme does not apply where the claimant is a litigant in person (45.7(3)).

Issued Proceedings

The scheme does not apply if proceedings have been issued, even if liability is admitted and it is only quantum that is in dispute.

Damage Only – No Injury

Such claims are covered provided the small claims track limit of £5,000 is exceeded.

Credit Hire

Credit hire is covered subject to the appropriate small claims track limit being exceeded.

Children and Patients

Claims brought on behalf of children or patients (as defined in Part 21 of the Civil Procedure Rules) are covered.

Part 45.10, dealing with the recoverability of disbursements, specifically allows recovery of certain disbursements, namely counsel's fees and court fees on an application to the court, "where they are necessarily incurred by reason of one or more of the claimants being a child or patient as defined in Part 21."

Thus the Rules envisage cases involving children or patients as being covered by the scheme.

Motor Insurers' Bureau Claims

The fixed recoverable costs scheme applies to uninsured drivers' cases but not to untraced drivers' cases (Practice Direction Relating to Part 45, 25A.4).

For the separate contingency fee scheme in relation to untraced drivers – see Chapter 6 – The Motor Insurers' Bureau Contingency Fee Scheme.

Date of Accidents

The fixed recoverable costs scheme is not retrospective. It covers only those accidents occurring on or after 6 October 2003. (25A.1 of Practice Direction.)

Multiple Claimants

Section 25A.7 of the Practice Direction states:

> Where there is more than one claimant in relation to a dispute and two or more claimants instruct the same solicitor or firm of solicitors, the provisions of the section apply in respect of each claimant.

Thus multiple claimants *are* covered and the solicitor receives a separate fixed fee in relation to each claimant.

This section suggests, by implication, that if separate firms are instructed then the scheme does not apply. However that is not how Part 45.7 reads and I believe that this is simply bad wording in the Practice Direction.

There would be no logic in one firm being able to get five separate fixed fees for acting in the same case but separate firms being denied the fixed fee. It is of course cost-neutral to the defendant – a fixed fee is a fixed fee, whoever it is paid to.

Provided each claimant's claim exceeds the small claims limit but does not exceed the £10,000 limit then *all* are covered. Thus the fact that five people may have claims of £10,000 each, total £50,000, does not take the matter outside the fixed recoverable costs scheme.

If some are within the terms of the scheme and some are not then that is how they will be treated, that is some will attract fixed costs but not others. There is no requirement that *all* claimants' claims arising from one dispute must be within the scheme for *any* to be within it.

Example

Ann, Belinda and Catherine are all injured in the same accident. The only claim is for damages for personal injury and their general damages are valued as follows:–

Ann   750.00

Belinda   4,000.00

Catherine   15,000.00

Ann is outwith the scheme as the claim would normally have been allocated to the small claims track.

Belinda will attract a fixed fee (£1,600).

Catherine is outwith the scheme as her damages exceed £10,000.

Multi-Track Claims

A claim which may have been allocated to the multi-track is nevertheless covered by the scheme. It will be rare for a claim that would have been allocated to the multi-track to satisfy the other conditions of the scheme but it is possible.

For example an accident involving a large number of claimants with relatively low-level injuries – the Liverpool bus with 683 people on board or the Luton taxi with 85 people in – (joke! joke!) – may have been allocated to the multi-track but if the claims are settled pre-issue for £10,000 or less then the fixed recoverable costs scheme applies.

Part 45.7(2)(d) provides that the section applies where "if a claim had been issued for the amount of the agreed damages, the small claims track would not have been the normal track for that claim".

Thus claims which would have been allocated to the multi-track are within the scope of the fixed recoverable costs scheme in the same way as claims that would have been allocated to the fast track.

Similarly a claim which, because of its gross value may have been allocated to the multi-track, will be within the scheme if the agreed damages are £10,000 or less.

Example 1

Full value of claim	18,000.00
50% agreed contributory negligence	9,000.00
Agreed damages	9,000.00

Such a settlement is within the fixed recoverable costs scheme even though it may have been allocated to the multi-track if issued.

Example 2

Value of claim	18,000.00
CRU	9,000.00
Agreed balance	9,000.00

Such a settlement is within the fixed recoverable costs scheme even though it may have been allocated to the multi-track if issued.

Damages

As we have seen it is a requirement that "the total value of the agreed damages does not exceed £10,000" (45.7(2)(c)).

What then are damages?

Damages *include* general damages and special damages and interest and interim payments (P.D. 25A.3(a)(b)).

Damages do *not* include any sum attributed to contributory negligence (P.D. 25A.3(c)).

Example

Claim at full value	18,000.00
Agreed 50% deduction for contributory negligence	9,000.00
Damages for purposes of fixed costs	9,000.00

Thus although the *claim* was £18,000 the settlement figure ("agreed damages") is within the scheme and will attract a fixed fee of £2,400.00.

Damages do *not* include any amount required by statute to be paid by the compensating party directly to a third party (such as sums paid by way of compensation recovery payment (CRU) and National Health Service expenses) (P.D. 25A.3(d)).

Example

Claim at full value	18,000.00
CRU	9,000.00
	—————
Damages for fixed costs purposes	9,000.00
	—————

Thus although the *claim* was £18,000 the deemed settlement figure is within the scheme and will attract a fixed fee of £2,400.

The Golden Ring

Rule 45.9(2) Civil Procedure Rules reads:–

"(2) Where the claimant –

(a) lives or works in an area set out in the relevant practice direction; and

(b) instructs a solicitor or firm of solicitors who practise in that area,

the fixed recoverable costs shall include, in addition to the costs specified in paragraph (1), an amount equal to 12.5% of the costs allowable under that paragraph."

Paragraph 25A.6 of the Practice Direction relating to Part 45 provides that the areas referred to in Rule 45.9(2), and thus forming the "golden ring" are the county court districts of Barnet, Bow, Brentford, Central London, Clerkenwell, Edmonton, Ilford, Lambeth, Mayors and City of London, Romford, Shoreditch, Wandsworth, West London, Woolwich and (outside London) the county court districts of Bromley, Croydon, Dartford, Gravesend and Uxbridge.

Note that the *claimant* must live or work in the golden ring and thus crafty law firms cannot simply gain the enhancement by opening a tiny office in the golden ring.

Even where the claimant does live or work in the golden ring the enhancement will only be gained if the solicitor practises in the golden ring as well.

For the purposes of calculating the recoverable success fee in conditional fee cases the relevant base fee is the *unenhanced* fee.

Thus whether a golden ring firm and client or not the success fee will be the same. This is because of the Civil Procedure (Amendment No. 5) Rules 2003 (Statutory Instrument 2003 No. 3361 (L.38)), Paragraph 9 of which provides:–

> "9.   In rule 45.11, for paragraph (2) substitute –
>
> > "(2) The amount of the success fee shall be 12.5% of the fixed recoverable costs calculated in accordance with rule 45.9(1), disregarding any additional amount which may be included in the fixed recoverable costs by virtue of rule 45.9(2)."

See also Chapter 3 – Fixed Costs and Conditional Fees.

The Escape Clause

Rule 45.12 reads:–

Claims for an amount of costs exceeding fixed recoverable costs

> 45.12   (1) The court will entertain a claim for an amount of costs (excluding any success fee or disbursements) greater than the fixed recoverable costs but only if it considers

that there are exceptional circumstances making it appropriate to do so.

(2) If the court considers such a claim appropriate, it may –

    (a) assess the costs; or

    (b) make an order for the costs to be assessed.

(3) If the court does not consider the claim appropriate, it must make an order for fixed recoverable costs only.

Failure to achieve costs greater than fixed recoverable costs

45.13 (1) This rule applies where –

    (a) costs are assessed in accordance with rule 45.12(2); and

    (b) the court assesses the costs (excluding any VAT) as being an amount which is less than 20% greater than the amount of the fixed recoverable costs.

(2) The court must order the defendant to pay the claimant the lesser of –

    (a) the fixed recoverable costs; and

    (b) the assessed costs.

Costs of the costs-only proceedings

45.14 Where –

> (a) the court makes an order for fixed recoverable costs in accordance with 45.12(3); or
>
> (b) rule 45.13 applies,
>
> the court must –
>
> (i) make no award for the payment of the claimant's costs in bringing the proceedings under rule 44.12A; and
>
> (ii) order that the claimant pay the defendant's costs of defending those proceedings."

This is achieved by the Civil Procedure (Amendment No. 4) Rules 2003 which introduced the whole concept of fixed recoverable costs in road traffic accident cases which settle pre-issue for £10,000.00 or less.

The explanatory note reads:–

> "– Section II of Part 45, which introduces a scheme providing that only specified fixed costs are to be recoverable, other than in exceptional circumstances, where costs-only proceedings are issued under rule 44.12A in relation to disputes arising out of road traffic accidents occurring on or after 6 October 2003 which are settled for an amount of agreed damages not exceeding £10,000.00."

Thus it will be seen that there are two hurdles to overcome in order to escape fixed costs.

Firstly it will be necessary to persuade the court that there are exceptional circumstances making it appropriate for the court to entertain a claim for an amount of costs greater than the fixed recoverable costs (Rule 45.12(1)).

If the court is satisfied that there are exceptional circumstances then it may assess the costs there and then or make an order for the costs to be assessed at a future hearing (Rule 45.12(2)).

If the court does not consider it appropriate to entertain such a claim then it must make an order for fixed recoverable costs only, that is no more and no less (Rule 45.12(3)).

In these circumstances a court must make no award for the payment of the claimant's costs in bringing the proceedings under Rule 44.12A (Rule 45.14(b)(i)) and must also order that the claimant pay the defendant's costs of defending those proceedings (Rule 45.14(b)(ii)).

Thus the court has no discretion on this part of the costs issue – if it refuses to entertain a claim under the "escape clause" then it must order costs against the claimant.

This is noteworthy. It is extremely rare for parliament to allow a court no discretion whatsoever in relation to a costs issue, but here that is exactly what parliament has done, no doubt to discourage strongly any attempt by claimant's solicitors to escape the fixed costs regime.

Even further if the claimant's solicitor is successful in obtaining an order under Rule 45.12(2) there is a further hurdle to overcome.

In order to avoid the adverse costs consequences set out above the court must assess a claimant's costs, excluding any VAT, as being 20% or more greater than the amount of the fixed recoverable costs (Rule 45.13(1)(b)).

If the court assesses the costs at less than 20% of the fixed recoverable costs then the court must order the defendant to pay the claimant the lesser of –

(a) the fixed recoverable costs; and

(b) the assessed costs

Example 1

Fixed recoverable costs would be £1,000.

The claimant's solicitor succeeds under Rule 45.12 and the court assesses the costs at £1,150.

Even though the claimant's solicitor has exceeded fixed costs by £150, or 15%, he or she has fallen foul of Rule 45.13 in that the sum assessed by the court is less than 20% greater than the amount of the fixed recoverable costs.

The court must order the fixed recoverable costs, i.e. £1,000 and also must order the claimant to pay the defendant's costs of defending those proceedings.

Example 2

Fixed recoverable costs would be £3,000.

The claimant's solicitor succeeds under Rule 45.12 but on assessment the court assesses the costs at £2,600.

The court must order only £2,600 even though fixed recoverable costs would have been £3,000 as it has to award the lesser of the two (Rule 45.13(2)). The court must also order the claimant to pay the defendant's costs of defending those proceedings.

Note that if the court orders an amount 20% or more greater than the fixed recoverable costs then the claimant's solicitor gets that sum but the court does not have to order the defendant to pay the claimant's costs of bringing the costs only proceedings.

It can safely be assumed that orders allowing costs greater than fixed recoverable costs will be very rare indeed.

Unless the defendant's misconduct has been very serious indeed my advice is not to seek to utilise the escape clause.

CHAPTER 2
FIXED COSTS OR CAPPED COSTS?

CHAPTER 2
FIXED COSTS OR CAPPED COSTS?

The new regime is a *fixed* costs regime and not a *capped* costs regime and this is a crucial difference.

Capped costs are just that – the costs are capped but a receiving party still has to show that work has been done to the value claimed, whereas fixed costs are, well, fixed no matter how little or how much work has been done.

Thus capped costs represent a *maximum* figure for the work done whereas fixed costs represent the actual figure that will be received and thus fixed costs are both a maximum and a minimum.

Those of you old enough to remember Scale Costs in County Court proceedings (abolished by the Civil Procedure Rules in 1999) will have no difficulty understanding the concept of capped costs.

The crucial difference between the two is that with fixed costs there is no need to justify the amount of work done *nor who it was done by* and thus the old costs negotiators' argument that the work should have been done by a Grade 12 fee-earner being an occupant of the office crèche is redundant.

(For a classic example of confusion over the difference between fixed costs and capped costs see Chapter 8: The Court of Protection).

Any Problems?

So is that it? You just do the work, forget about time-recording, grades of fee-earner, etc.? Well not quite.

The problem, an entirely unnecessary one, is that you can never guarantee that the case will not have to be issued, whereupon all pre-issue work, as well as post-issue work, ceases to be covered by the fixed costs regime. Then it will be necessary to show how long the work took and what grade of fee-earner carried out the work.

This is the major flaw of the new scheme and it is a major flaw indeed.

The answer is to say that whatever ultimately happens in the case the pre-issue element of costs is fixed as per the table of fees. Thus on, say, a £5,000 claim (fixed fee £1,800) one would simply carry that fee into the issued litigation and the loser would pay the winner £1,800 in respect of pre-issue costs.

The argument against this is that the cases that have to be issued will, by definition, have involved the most pre-issue work and are therefore not suitable for fixed costs. However the scheme is meant to be a "swings and roundabouts" one with some cases settling very early and some settling just pre-issue.

The level of fees is sufficient to cover all pre-issue work, whether the case is actually issued or not. After all we are only talking about road traffic accident cases involving £10,000 or less.

The potentially serious problem about this flaw is that it will encourage solicitors to work in the same old way.

We all know that the non-fixed fee method of working, that is the hourly rate, favours Messrs. Dawdle, Dither and Drag-it-out over Messrs. Sharpe and Quick.

Fixed fees and contingency fees have the opposite effect.

It is obviously difficult to plan a practice and to design a system of working if one is never sure whether the piece of work one is doing will fall to be paid on an hourly rate basis or by a fixed fee.

Example

Two people each have an accident, in relation to which the facts and law etc. are for all purposes identical.

Each claim is worth £3,000 (fixed fee £1,400).

Messrs. Dawdle Dither and Drag-it-out carry on in their own antiquated way and do 15 hours pre-issue work (including letters and telephones etc.).

Messrs. Sharpe and Quick, computerised and efficient, carry out the work in 6 hours.

Both utilise Grade 1 fee-earners allowed at £170.00 per hour by the local court.

Result

(1) Case not issued.

Dawdle's fees   £1,400.00

Sharpe's fees   £1,400.00

Fixed fee in each case.

(2) Case issued

Fees for pre-issue work

Dawdle's fees   £2,550.00   (£170 × 15 hours)

Sharpe's fees   £1,020.00   (£170 × 6 hours)

Variance as against fixed fee

Dawdle: +   £1,150.00

Sharpe: −   £380.00

Thus even the most forward-thinking firms may be reluctant to go the whole hog with computerisation and efficiency as they will be punished if the case has to be issued.

It is ironic that liability insurers fear that solicitors will try and issue anything that they can so as to avoid fixed costs, and thus get higher fees, and efficient solicitors fear that if they are forced into issuing (because, for example, quantum cannot be agreed) then they will receive a *lower* fee than if the case had been settled pre-issue.

Thus the only winner is the inefficient solicitor. (What's new there then?)

Liability insurers and efficient claimant solicitors should work together to drive out the inefficient firms. However that has not happened in the last 1,000 years so I am not holding my breath.

Solutions

1.   Change the law so that whatever ultimately happens in the case the pre-issue element of costs is fixed; or

2.   Amend the rules to provide that where a case is issued the assessed fee in respect of pre-issue work shall never be less than the fixed fee for such work had the case settled pre-issue. This would allow a higher, but not a lower, fee than fixed costs and thus the efficient solicitor would not be punished for being efficient.

I favour solution 1 for reasons already set out.

Solution 2 only partly levels the playing field. In the example given above the fees would now be as follows:

Case Issued

Fees for pre-issue work

Dawdle's fees   £2,550.00   (£170 × 15 hours)

Sharpe's fees   £1,400.00   (Fixed fee)

Under solution 1 both firms would receive £1,400, irrespective of work done.

Solution 1 has the additional benefit of removing any need for assessment in respect of pre-issue work in any road traffic case involving £10,000 or less, and would make the completion of the costs estimate in the allocation questionnaire much simpler.

What should I do?

Take the modern approach. Dawdle, Dither and Drag-it-out will die anyway.

Accept that on the odd issued case you may lose out because of your efficiency but remember that you will be benefiting on all of the unissued cases and you will be well-prepared for the future.

Overall liability insurers like fixed fees and are unlikely to cause the same problems that they caused with the recoverability of success fees and insurance premia.

Trust me. I am a lawyer.

CHAPTER 3
FIXED COSTS AND CONDITIONAL FEES

CHAPTER 3
FIXED COSTS AND CONDITIONAL FEES

As we have seen the fixed recoverable costs regime currently applies only to unissued road traffic accident cases with a value of £10,000.00, or less.

There was never any doubt that such cases conducted under a conditional fee agreement, or a collective conditional fee agreement, attracted a success fee over and above the fixed costs, nor that that success fee would be expressed as a percentage of the fixed fee.

The key issue was as to the *level* of such a success fee. That, too, has now been fixed.

With effect from 1 March 2004 all cases covered by the fixed recoverable costs scheme and conducted under a conditional fee agreement or a collective conditional fee agreement attract a fixed success fee of 12.5% of the base fee. The base fee includes both the core fee of £800.00 and the contingency fee element of 20% up to £5,000.00 and 15% of the damages between £5,000.00 and £10,000.00.

This is achieved by the Civil Procedure (Amendment No. 5) Rules 2003 (Statutory Instrument 2003 No. 3361 (L.38)), Paragraph 9 of which provides:

"9. In rule 45.11, for paragraph (2) substitute –

"(2) The amount of the success fee shall be 12.5% of the fixed recoverable costs calculated in accordance with rule 45.9(1), disregarding any additional amount which may be included in the fixed recoverable costs by virtue of rule 45.9(2).".

Golden Ring

By Paragraph 1(b) Rule 9 came into effect on 1st March 2004. Rule 45.9 (2) refers to the "golden ring"[1] enhancement – see below.

---

1. *The "golden ring"*

    Rule 45.9(2) Civil Procedure Rules reads:

    "(2) Where the claimant –

    (a) lives or works in an area set out in the relevant practice direction; and

    (b) instructs a solicitor or firm of solicitors who practise in that area,

    the fixed recoverable costs shall include, in addition to the costs specified in paragraph (1), an amount equal to 12.5% of the costs allowable under that paragraph."

    Paragraph 25A.6 of the Practice Direction relating to Part 45 provides that the areas referred to in Rule 45.9(2), and thus forming the "golden ring" are the county court districts of Barnet, Bow, Brentford, Central London, Clerkenwell, Edmonton, Ilford, Lambeth, Mayors and City of London, Romford, Shoreditch, Wandsworth, West London, Woolwich and (outside London) the county court districts of Bromley, Croydon, Dartford, Gravesend and Uxbridge.

Example

Ian Injured is represented by his solicitors under a conditional fee agreement and the case is settled for £8,000.00 pre-issue.

	£.	£.
Fixed costs		2,250.00
(Comprised core fee	800.00	
20% of first 5,000	1,000.00	
15% of balance of 3,000	450.00	
	2,250.00)	
12.5% success fee on *total*		281.25
Total solicitors' costs		
(excluding VAT and disbursements)		2,531.25

Thus the calculation becomes a little bit complicated, especially if you are in the "golden ring" and already receive an enhancement of 12.5% when the calculation for Ian Injured is as follows:–

	£	£
Standard fixed costs		2,250.00
(Comprised core fee	800.00	
20% of first 5,000	1,000.00	
15% of balance of 3,000	450.00	
Unenhanced fee	2,250.00)	
12.5% golden ring enhancement		281.25
		2,531.25
12.5% success fee on *unenhanced* fee only		281.25
Total solicitors' costs		
(excluding VAT and disbursements)		2,812.50

The 12.5% fixed success fee is on the unenhanced, rather than the enhanced figure because the new Rule 45.11, inserted by Paragraph 9 of The Civil Procedure (Amendment No. 5) Rules 2003 (see above) states that the golden ring enhancement shall be disregarded when determining the base fee to which the 12.5% fixed success fee applies.

The effect of this is that in a golden ring case with a fixed success fee the solicitor's costs will be 25% above the normal, base costs as demonstrated in the example above.

Never fear. I have done all of the calculations for you in the next chapter, Chapter 4: Ready Reckoners. This contains six tables:–

Table 1	Standard Rate	–	no success fee
Table 2	Standard Rate	–	12.5% success fee
Table 3	Standard Rate	–	20% success fee
Table 4	Enhanced Rate	–	no success fee
Table 5	Enhanced Rate	–	12.5% success fee
Table 6	Enhanced Rate	–	20% success fee.

As stated above this came into effect on 1 March 2004 and there will be a limited pool of cases to which the fixed costs regime applies but to which the fixed success fee does *not* apply.

These are cases where the cause of action arose on or after 6 October 2003 and where a conditional fee agreement was entered into on or before 29 February 2004, or the case was taken on by a solicitor under the aegis of a collective conditional agreement on or before 29 February 2004.

Theoretically the court's assessment of the success fee in such cases is carried out in exactly the same manner as in any other case. Clearly if the case has been correctly "called" at the beginning as a straightforward road traffic accident case where proceedings were unlikely to be necessary then it will fall on all fours with *Callery* v *Gray* where a 20% success fee was allowed by the House of Lords.

However in *Callery* v *Gray* both the Court of Appeal and the House of Lords left open the opportunity for the Court of Appeal to revisit the level of success fees as more information came to light and as everyone gained more experience of this type of case.

Thus it may be that the courts will take the view, that in the light of such experience, 12.5% is the appropriate figure. The difference between the two figures of 12.5% and 20% is not great in cash terms.

You can work out what the difference is in any given case by comparing the costs inclusive of a 12.5% success fee (Table 2) and the costs inclusive of a 20% success fee (Table 3).

Example

Tracey Transitional was injured on 15 October 2003 and the conditional fee agreement was signed the next day. The case settles pre-issue for £3,000.00.

	£
Table 3 (20% success fee) costs	1,680.00
Table 2 (12.5% success fee) costs	1,575.00
Difference	105.00

Another way of calculating the difference – which is always 7.5% of base costs – is to look at the figure without any success fee (*Table 1*) and then take 7.5% of that figure.

Example As Above

Settlement pre-issue at £3,000.00.

	£
Table 1 (no success fee) costs	1,400.00
Difference = 7.5% thereof	105.00

On the standard fixed costs the minimum difference (on a settlement of £1,000.01) is £75.00 (£1,125.00 compared with £1,200.00) and the maximum difference (on a settlement of £10,000.00) is £191.25 (£2,868.75 compared with £3,060.00).

The position in relation to Golden Ring cases is exactly the same since the success fee is based on the *unenhanced* rule and *not* the *enhanced* rule.

Splitting the difference might be a good idea!

Success Fee Fixed In All Road Traffic Accident Cases Under £500,000.00

Yes that's right. Amazing but true!

With effect, probably from 1 June 2004, in all road traffic accident cases worth £500,000.00 or less, the solicitor's success fee will be fixed at 12.5% for cases that settle and 100% for those that reach trial.

Trial is likely to be defined as anything other than a procedural hearing and this will include disposal hearings, that is hearings dealing with damages only.

All of this will be achieved by statutory instrument, later in 2004. Check the HMSO website for Civil Procedure (Amendment) Rules SI's.

Even for cases involving more than £500,000.00 the starting point is that there will be a 12.5% success fee as above but there will be an escape clause in such cases allowing for a potentially higher success fee than 12.5% on settlement.

In practice cases of such high value are few and far between and therefore from a practice management point of view it can be assumed that the success fee will now be fixed in all road traffic cases.

Unsurprisingly I have not prepared tables for unlimited, unfixed costs but the principle is the same and thus an agreement in transitional cases over whether the success fee should be 12.5% or 20% will be an argument over a figure equal to 7.5% of base costs, but of course if base costs are, say, £100,000.00 that is a difference of £7,500.00 and not the relatively insignificant difference arising on the success fee on fixed costs.

Potentially the argument could be over a much greater sum.

Example

A posh client, Charles Catastrophically-Injured, is involved in a road traffic accident on 11 October 2003.

Initially sparring with the liability insurers indicates that they will contest the matter and on 12 April 2004 the claimant and his solicitor enter into a conditional fee agreement with a 100% success fee. In June 2006, shortly before trial, the case settles for £500,000.00.

Base costs are agreed at £100,000.00. The defendants argue for a fixed success fee of 12.5% but the claimant's solicitor argues for 100% as the matter was obviously high risk as it only settled just before trial.

	£
Success fee if claimant's argument succeeds	100,000.00
Success fee if defendant's argument succeeds	12,500.00
Difference	87,500.00

Of course if Charles Catastrophically-Injured entered into the conditional fee agreement on 1 June 2004 (assuming that is when the new Rules come in) then there would be no argument – the success fee would be fixed at 12.5% with no escape.

The low success fee of 12.5% fails to take into account the real risk to a solicitor of carrying out a great deal of work for nothing in high-value cases and also fails to take into account the risk of failing to beat a Part 36 offer.

Cashflow Element Of Success Fee

The solicitor is still free to charge the client the cashflow element of the success fee, that is the element relating to the *delay* in payment, rather than the risk of *not being paid at all*. This is certainly the case in reflection to non-fixed costs cases and possibly in relation to fixed costs cases.

Now that the success fee recoverable from the other side is likely to be very low in virtually all cases, and with interest rates rising, it is time to put in a higher figure for cashflow. I suggest 20% in all cases. With the recoverable element being fixed conditional fee agreements are unlikely ever to see the light of day, and a deal can always be done with a complaining client.

Unless the Rules, relating to non-fixed costs cases, not yet published, deal with the issue then the cashflow element is chargeable on the *solicitor and own client* rate, although the *recoverable* success fee is likely to be a percentage uplift on between-the-parties costs and not, as at present, on solicitor and own client costs.

However in relation to the success fee on fixed costs cases, that is only road traffic accident cases settled pre-issue for

£10,000.00 or less, it is arguable that no cashflow element can be charged as the new rule 45.11(2) reads:

> "The amount of the success fee shall be 12.5% of the fixed recoverable costs..."

However the Explanatory Notes to the Civil Procedure (Amendment No. 5) Rules 2003 state:

> "Rule 45.11 is amended to specify the amount of the success fee which a claimant may *recover* (my emphasis) in proceedings under Section II of Part 45 if he has entered into a conditional fee agreement or a collective conditional fee agreement which provides for a success fee."

That suggests that the fixing of the success fee is in relation to only the recoverable element. Of course the original conditional fee agreeement must contain a statement as to the cashflow element because the Conditional Fee Agreements Regulations 2000 require it and when you enter into a C.F.A. you do not know that it will end up being a fixed costs case. My advice is to put a 20% cashflow element in with conditional fee cases which are likely to settle.

Example

Settlement at £30,000.00.

	£
Agreed recoverable costs	14,000.00
Recoverable success fee (12.5%)	1,750.00

Actual work done:

80 hours at £220.00 = £17,600.00

20% cash flow on 17,600.00 = £3,520.00.

This may be charged whether or not the solicitor chooses to charge the client the difference between the solicitor and own client fee at the recoverable costs.

Counsel

Barristers will be subject to the same fixed success fee regime as solicitors in road traffic accident cases save that an extra tier has been added for cases that settle shortly before trial. Thus barristers, but only barristers, will receive a 75% success fee when a road traffic accident case settles within 21 days of a multi-track trial and a 50% success fee when such a case settles within 14 days of a fast-track trial.

In cases covered by the fixed *costs* regime, that is cases settled pre-issue for £10,000.00 or less, counsel's fees, and any success fee thereon, come out of the solicitor's fixed fee together with any fixed success fee thereon.

Part 11.8

As we all know the Practice Direction About Costs, Supplementing Parts 43 to 48 of the Civil Procedure Rules, Part 11.8, gives the court power to allow a higher success fee, recoverable from the other side, if the legal representative takes liability for any disbursements, that is neither charges the client for them nor takes out after-the-event insurance in relation to them.

Thus the solicitor who saves the cost of after-the-event insurance gets a success fee enhancement, which in our experience is around 10%. Thus in a typical *Callery* v *Gray* type case we would expect a 30% success fee as we do not insure, or rather we self-insure. Everyone has been happy with this as it costs the liability insurers significantly less than the recoverable after-the-event insurance premium, which they detest in any event.

What is to happen now under the fixed success fee regime? Clearly there is no problem with the 100% success fee on cases that go to trial as 100% is an absolute maximum that cannot be added to.

The problem is with the 12.5% fixed success fee which would appear not to allow a Part 11.8 addition. If the self-insuring solicitor is to obtain no enhancement for the extra risk he or she may decide to abandon that policy and to take out after-the-event insurance.

Assuming the Part 11.8 addition never exceeds 10% of base costs it can never exceed £255.00 in standard cases (10% of £2,550.00 – being the highest fixed fee – on a settlement of £10,000.00).

As the after-the-event insurance premia virtually always exceed even the maximum sum this is a waste of liability insurers' money with no benefit going to the claimant's solicitor.

True the 10% extra becomes a greater sum in the fixed success fee regime beyond the fixed *costs* regime, that is *all* road traffic accident cases, but the after-the-event insurance premium will also be much higher.

In any event the vast majority of claims are for £10,000.00 or under and are thus caught by the fixed costs regime.

The answer is to allow a fixed sum for disbursements, of say £500.00, in fixed *costs* cases and let the solicitor insure or not as they wish.

(Part 11.8 reads:

11.8 (1) In deciding whether a percentage increase is reasonable relevant factors to be taken into account may include:–

(a) the risk that circumstances in which the costs, fees or expenses would be payable might not occur;

(b) the legal representative's liability for any disbursements;

(c) what other methods of financing the costs were available to the receiving party.)

Part 11.8 has not been altered by the latest rule change.

Notional Insurance Premia

Those organisations enjoying Membership Organisation status are still able to recover a notional insurance premium in fixed costs cases. The original Part 45.10(2)(b) referred to "the amount of an insurance premium" but the latest amendments to the Civil Procedure Rules have clarified this point to confirm that Membership Organisations may still recover a notional insurance premium.

Paragraph 8 of The Civil Procedure (Amendment No. 5) Rules 2003 (Statutory Instrument 2003 No. 3361 (L. 38) reads:

"8. In rule 45.10(2), in sub-paragraph (b), at the end insert –

"or, where a body of a prescribed description within the meaning of section 30(1) of the Access to Justice Act 1999 undertakes to meet liabilities incurred to pay the costs of other parties to proceedings, a sum not exceeding such additional amount of costs as would be allowed under section 30 in respect of provision made against the risk of having to meet such liabilities;"

The explanatory notes provide:

Rule 45.10 is amended to clarify that, in costs-only proceedings brought under Section II of Part 45 by a party funded by a body which indemnifies its members or other persons against liabilities for costs which they may incur in proceedings, the court may allow that party as a disbursement a sum not exceeding such amount as would be allowed under section 30 of the Access to Justice Act 1999.

The Conditional Fee Agreement In Practice

It is vital to note that in fixed costs cases conducted under a conditional fee agreement the full rigours and technicalities of the Conditional Fee Agreements Regulations and the Conditional Fee Agreements Order apply without any mitigation whatsoever.

Sorry, but there it is.

The indemnity principle also applies in full and without mitigation, unless you utilize CFA-lite. I have neither seen nor heard of a single CFA-lite agreement in practice so I will assume the use of a CFA Mark 2, that is the post 1st April 2000 model.

This needs to be changed as the standard agreement risks a breach of the indemnity principle.

Example

Standard conditional fee agreement used. 6 hours work done at £180.00 per hour. Entitlement to costs under the indemnity principle = £1,080 (£180.00 × 6).

Settlement for £5,000.

Fixed cost – £1,800.

Claimant's solicitor's costs limited to £1,080 plus success fee.

Thus the conditional fee agreements, together with any Practice Rule 15 letter, must make the client liable to pay the *higher* of the fixed cost sum or the sum reached by utilising the hourly rate.

This is absolutely crucial. Failure to do so will result in failure to recover the fixed cost.

Failure to include entitlement to charge the *higher* of the two rates leads to problems if the case is issued.

Example

Solicitor has contractual right to fixed costs only.

10 hours pre-issue work done at £180.00.

Case issued and settled for £1,000.01. Indemnity principle limits fee to fixed costs – £1,000.00, instead of £1,800.00 (£180.00 × 10 hours).

Level Of Success Fee

I suggest 100% success fee in all cases, comprised of 20% cashflow element (see above) and 80% risk-based element which is the potentially recoverable element.

If the case is settled then, whatever the value and whatever has gone into the conditional fee agreement the claimant solicitor will get 12.5% (plus cashflow subject to the discussion above) and therefore nothing is lost and it saves making a calculation each time.

Of course the high figure has to go in any event to justify the 100% success fee if the case goes to trial. Note that in such circumstances only 80% will be payable by the other side as the overall maximum success fee remains at 100% and if 20% is utilised as a cashflow element then only the remainder – 80% – is recoverable from the other side.

For the solicitor it is better to get the 20% cashflow element in the vast majority of cases, which will settle, but the client who has won *at trial* may be unhappy when he or she learns that the *whole* 100% would have been recoverable from the other side had the conditional fee agreement been worded differently. If a case is obviously high-value and risky it may be wise to go for a 0%–100% split to avoid this.

Clearly a 20%–80% split in a case won at trial represents a windfall to the defendant, or rather his or her liability insurers.

Surely the time has come to fix *all* elements of the success fee (and experts' fees for that matter).

The Future

As costs become fixed in progressively more cases then conditional fees are likely to disappear as the extra element related to risk will be incorporated into the standard fee.

After all is there now a single solicitor in the country doing claimant personal injury work and getting paid in full in the event of defeat?[2]

---

2. OK, yes there is. The occasional client with legal expenses insurance who instructs a non-panel solicitor who manages to persuade the legal expenses insurer to fund the case win or lose. It does not happen very often!

All claimant personal injury work is now done on a conditional fee basis, whether it be trade union work, legal expenses insurance or whatever. The difference is between those who get a success fee and those who take the risk for no extra fee in return for a regular supply of work from an insurer, trade union etc.

Income Tax

This section proceeds on the basis that in reality virtually all claimant personal injury work is done on a conditional fee or contingency fee basis, whether or not a formal conditional fee agreement or collective conditional fee agreement is entered into.

We are now dealing with the Inland Revenue's rules and not the technicalities of valid conditional fee agreements. Thus a solicitor acting under legal expenses insurance who will only be paid in the event of a win, or a solicitor acting for a trade union member on the same basis, is entitled to the tax benefits set out below.

Fixed recoverable costs do nothing to alter the position and neither do fixed recoverable success fees in fixed costs cases (in force 1 March 2004) nor fixed recoverable success fees in all other road traffic accident cases.

It is the lack of certainty of being entitled to charge a fee that creates the tax advantage. Read on!

The Finance Act 1998 abolished the cash basis of income taxation for the professions and thus solicitors and barristers have to pay income tax on a realistic assessment of work in progress rather than paying income tax in the tax year in which the money is received.

In any event new firms of solicitors have been taxed on the work in progress basis for some time thus giving the old established firms an unfair tax advantage over young firms. All firms now have to calculate their profits for tax on a "true and fair" basis.

Note that there are different rules for barristers. Section 43, Finance Act 1998 allows barristers to compute their profits for tax purposes on a cash basis for periods of account ending not more than seven years after they first commence in practice.

The new rules came into effect on 6 April 1999 and thus applied to the first accounts year starting after that date. So for a business with a 30 April 1999 year end the new rules have been in operation since 1 May 1999 and the first set of accounts caught by the new rules were those for the year ending 30 April 2000.

Thus all work done, but not paid for, whether billed or not, had in theory to be brought into the accounts and tax paid on it. This would have resulted in huge tax bills for some firms and thus this catch-up charge is being spread over a ten-year period. This period commenced with the tax year 1999/2000 with the first payment of tax on this charge being made on 31 January 2001, the second on 31 January 2002, etc. This transitional regime will continue until the tax year 2008/2009 with the final transitional payment being made in 31 January 2010. After that everyone will be taxed on the same basis.

For a very useful article dealing with this change, but not conditional or contingency fees, see *"Taking advantage of new tax regulations"* by Hew Tittensor and Geoff Everett, *New Law Journal* Expert Witness Supplement 30 July 1999.

For young firms of solicitors none of this makes any difference as they have been taxed on this new basis anyway.

The question arises as to what work in progress exists in a conditional or contingency fee case. The Inland Revenue's very clear answer is "None" which is very good news for all those doing no win-no fee work.

Thus all firms will receive very significant tax advantages by working on a conditional or contingency fee basis as no tax is payable until the case is successfully concluded – at which point the fee should be received anyway.

Thus the old firms effectively remain on a cash basis and younger firms effectively move from a work-in-progress basis to a cash basis.

On a work-in-progress basis not all such work is taxed. A detailed explanation is beyond the scope of this chapter but for example partners' work is not included and staff time is at the cost to the business rather than the charging rate to the client, although it is now proposed to bring partners' work into account as taxable work-in-progress (see below).

The cost to the business will include the gross salary of the fee-earner and *may* include other direct costs such as secretarial support, rent and occupancy costs – in other words a share of the overheads. (See paragraphs 25–29 Inland Revenue Guidance Note – "Withdrawal of Cash Basis".)

Let us take an assistant solicitor doing claimant personal injury work. She has 150 files which will eventually, over a period of time, be billed out at £300,000. She is on average half way through the work and it thus has a billable value of £150,000.

As a rough and ready measure we will discount that by two-thirds leaving a cost price of £50,000. Tax at 40% on £50,000 = £20,000.

This would be the basis of the catch-up charge spread over 10 years but thereafter the new work will be taxed in real time, that is each year.

So if the solicitor is doing £150,000 worth of work a year and half is unbilled at the end of the year £75,000 is potentially taxable. Applying the two-thirds reduction tax will be charged on £25,000. 40% of £25,000 = £10,000.

Or take a new solicitor. She takes all the new personal injury work and at the end of the first year has billed nothing but has done £100,000 worth of work. Applying the two-thirds discount, tax will be charged on £34,000. 40% on £34,000 = £13,600.

This is very rough and ready but the Inland Revenue in its guidance note gives an extremely detailed example of an assistant solicitor's unbilled work of £135,000 having a net realisable value of £39,692 (a reduction of 70.6% compared with my 66.66%) with a consequent tax liability, at 40% of £15,876.80. (Annex D Example 3).

If all work on conditional fee basis = Nil.

The tax saving will depend upon the type of work. In employment, with a very rapid turnover, there will be less work in progress carried over but in personal injury work the savings are great because the work has a very slow turnover, often measured in years rather than weeks.

So why am I so confident that no tax is payable until the case is concluded?

Because the Inland Revenue say so. This whole area is dealt with in a Guidance Note prepared by the Tax Faculty of the Institute of Chartered Accountants and agreed by the Inland Revenue. It appeared in the Inland Revenue's Tax Bulletin of December 1998 at pages 606–615.

Work-in-progress has to be valued at the lower cost or "net realisable value" (NRV) and I have dealt in very broad terms with what this means for a non-conditional fee practice.

Paragraphs 36 of the Guidance Note says:–

> As with other judgments, the estimate of the net realisable value of work-in-progress should be made on the basis of the information available at the time the accounts are drawn up. Thus, where work is done on a speculative or contingency basis ("no win, no fee"), but it is clear at the time the accounts are drawn up that the case has been won and that the firm will at least recover its costs, work-in-progress on the contract should be valued at cost. Where, however, the contingency has not been satisfied at that time, so that there is still a reasonable chance that the firm will recover nothing, the net realisable value of work-in-progress is likely to be nil. Paragraph 49 also gives guidance on the recognition of income and contingent fee cases.

"But", I hear you say, "this requires "a reasonable chance that the firm will recover nothing" and that cannot be true in a field where most cases are won".

Well Paragraph 49 puts it beyond doubt.

> Paragraph 36 above discussed the treatment of contingent events in relation to work-in-progress. In the case of income recognition, the Revenue have told us that they accept that income need not be recognised for a job which depends on a contingency until that contingency is satisfied. For example, a lawyer who took on a case on a "no win, no fee" basis need not recognise the fee until the case is won; only then is the condition met which is necessary to earn the fee. In addition, the Revenue accept that, for this purpose, it is open to the professional to deal with a large number of similar cases either in the aggregate or to look at each one separately. Under the former approach it might be possible to say that a certain percentage will yield a fee and to recognise income accordingly.

Under the latter approach there is no certainty that any particular case will yield a fee and so no income need be recognised for any of them until the contingency is satisfied in each case.

The situation is the same for barristers. In a Revenue note for barristers, accompanying its Press Release of 22 December 1997, the Inland Revenue said

Conditional fee cases

No fees need to be brought into your accounts (and subjected to income tax) until the case has been won. The amount of the fee, if any, would remain uncertain until the case was won.

Thus conditional and contingency fee cases *delay* (but do not get rid of) income tax liability and will thus assist cash flow as far as income tax is concerned. This helps to offset the clear cashflow disadvantages of conditional and contingency fees.

Although work in progress is nil for income tax purposes banks and prospective partners will readily understand that conditional fee files do have a real work-in-progress value and thus it is possible to have the best of both worlds – work-in-progress with a genuine saleable or borrowing value but upon which no tax is paid until a later date.

This approach has been endorsed by the Chancery Division of the High Court in *Browell and Others* v *Goodyear* Times Law Reports 24 October 2000 where it was accepted that the value of work-in-progress, whilst nil for tax purposes, had a real value, in this case on the dissolution of a firm of solicitors.

This is an important case as it recognizes the apparently illogical concept of something having a realizable value in reality but not for tax purposes. Life is normally the other way round.

Browell involved the winding up of a five partner firm of solicitors and a dispute arose as to the valuation of work in progress with four of the partners seeking a declaration resisted by the fifth partner confirming the oft-expressed view that a solicitors' partnership is like a marriage but without the sex.

In this case the firm's work largely related to claims for damages for vibration white finger and chronic bronchitis and emphysema suffered by underground mineworkers and undertaken on a non win-no fee basis.

The claims were conducted in accordance with two claims handling agreements entered into with the Department of Trade and Industry and dated 22 January 1999 and 24 September 1999 respectively.

Under the schemes no costs were recoverable from the Department unless the claim succeeded, and there was an understanding that the firm would not attempt to recover costs in respect of unsuccessful claims from either the individual claimant or his trade union.

In successful cases a fixed amount of costs, dependent upon the complexity of the case, together with disbursements and VAT was recoverable from the Department.

In deciding the correct approach to any subsequent valuation the court was guided by three particular considerations:

(i) the method should be inexpensive and simple to apply;

(ii) the assessment would inevitably be inexact, since the work had not yet been completed and billed;

(iii) the benefit of doubt as to what would happen in a given event should be given to the party with the task of completing that work in progress as that party would be carrying the risk that the matter might never complete.

The High Court declined to follow the New Zealand case of *Robertson* v *Brent and Haggitt* [1972] New Zealand Law Reports 406 where Mr. Justice Wilson held that work in progress, at least in relation to professional services, had no value in that no payment was due from the client until the services had been rendered.

> While that method might be appropriate to the assessment of income for income tax purposes, different considerations applied here. The fact that no payment was due from the client until the services had been rendered in full did not mean that the work in progress in connection with those services had no value.

The method producing the fairest assessment involved establishing what percentage of the work in progress had already been completed as at the date of dissolution and then calculating, by reference to the total fee when completed, what sum had been earned up to dissolution.

The court said that even this method had to be approached with care. It was necessary to consider the claims as a whole to establish:

(i) the proportion likely to result in an accepted offer and therefore recovery of fees;

(ii) the proportion of the work done by the date of dissolution.

In summary the High Court said that the most appropriate way to estimate the value of work undertaken on a no win-no fee basis which was in progress at the time of dissolution of a firm of solicitors, having regard to considerations of time and costs, was to establish what proportion of a particular class of work was likely to be completed successfully and then establish what percentage of that work had already been completed by the firm at the date of dissolution.

The court was dealing with a dissolution but clearly this method of calculation could be used at any given time to establish the firm's work in progress value. Presented correctly these figures are a comfort to lenders and also to partners as it will demonstrate the true, underlying value of the business rather than the depressingly high overdraft figure familiar to no win-no fee practices.

It is vital that lawyers understand that conditional and contingency fee work in progress can be brought into play in the trading and management accounts without creating a premature income tax liability.

No win – lower fee

This still leaves open the question of "no win – lower fee" conditional fee agreements which are becoming increasingly common for commercial work and for defence personal injury work.

The contractual arrangement under such schemes may be along the lines of "£95.00 per hour in the event of defeat, £190.00 in the event of victory" with of course an appropriate success fee added to reflect the risks in the case of only receiving the lower fee (rather than the no fee payable in a no win-no fee case).

It seems to me that such work should be treated on the conventional basis for working on an hourly rate, namely that work in progress is brought in to calculation for income tax purposes, but only to the extent of the guaranteed hourly rate, £95.00 in this example, with the balance being treated as a conditional/contingency fee as set out above both for income tax and work in progress valuation purposes.

Cases concluded but no costs not yet agreed

My view is that these do not need to be brought into account for income tax purposes as there is, at this point, no entitlement to any fees and no absolute certainty of being awarded costs.

Costs agreed or ordered but not yet paid

These should be brought into account for tax purposes as the fee has become certain. If anything subsequently happens, for example a successful appeal against an order, then the appropriate adjustments can be made to the income tax return for the following year.

Taxing Partners' Work in Progress

As we have seen partners' work-in-progress does not need to be brought into account for income tax purposes, that is it is only taxed when a bill is delivered, in contrast to the work-in-progress of other members of staff.

In November 2003 changes in the way that all businesses account for revenue was introduced by the Accounting Standards Board (ASB) in an application note to FRS5, an official ruling applying to accounting periods ending on or after 23 December 2003.

The key change for law firms, including limited liability partnerships and companies, and barristers, is that the profit on equity partner time will be recognized, and therefore taxable, while the work is in progress and not, as is currently the case, when the bill has been delivered.

The changes will take effect in the current accounting year. Firms whose year end was 31 March 2004 will face a larger tax bill on 31 January 2005 and those whose year ended on 30 April 2004 will have until January 2006 to find the extra tax.

It is effectively a one-off revenue raising exercise as although work-in-progress will continue to be taxable it will not become taxable again when it is turned into bills and in any one year the two should roughly match. It is a "catching-up" charge that will hit hard in year one.

The good news is that none of this affects the position in relation to conditional fee work as it does not have to be brought into account, whoever it is done by. (See Paragraphs 36 and 49 of the Inland Revenue Guidance Note set out above.)

Thus the only effect on conditional and contingency fee firms is to give them a slight additional competitive edge over the next couple of years as other firms will be faced with a one-off significant extra tax charge but they will not.

Notional Insurance Premia: Taxable Income?

Part 45.10 of the Civil Procedure Rules reads:–

"Disbursements

45.10   (1) The court –

(a) may allow a claim for a disbursement of a type mentioned in paragraph (2); but

(b) must not allow a claim for any other type of disbursement.

> (2) The disbursements referred to in paragraph (1) are – ......
>
> (b) the amount of an insurance premium, or where a body of prescribed description within the meaning of section 30(1) of the Access to Justice Act 1999 undertakes to meet liabilities incurred to pay the costs of other parties to proceedings, a sum not exceeding such additional amount of costs as would be allowed under section 30 in respect of provision made against the risk of having to meet such liability."

To remind you, that part of Rule 45.10(2)(b) dealing with the notional insurance premium is new, having been inserted by the Civil Procedure (Amendment No. 5) Rules 2003, the explanatory note to which reads:–

> "Rule 45.10 is amended to clarify that, in costs-only proceedings brought under Section II of Part 45 by a party funded by a body which indemnifies its members or other persons against liabilities for costs which they may incur in proceedings, the court may allow that party as a disbursement a sum not exceeding such amount as would be allowed under section 30 of the Access to Justice Act 1999."

So is this "disbursement", which is never in fact disbursed, taxable income or not?

Clearly if an actual premium had been incurred and recovered there would be no tax payable. Why should it be any different for a notional premium, especially when the rule and the explanatory note refer to it as a "disbursement"?

For firms doing Membership Organisation work notional premia add up and the tax or lack of it will be a very substantial sum.

My view is that it is taxable income and is wrongly described as a disbursement. Rather it is an enhancement of the solicitor's fee for taking extra risk.

CHAPTER 4
READY RECKONERS

CHAPTER 4
READY RECKONERS

Table 1 gives the fixed costs figure, without a success fee, in respect of each band of £100 between the minimum cost-bearing award of damages (£1,000) to the limit of damages covered by the fixed fee scheme (£10,000).

The actual scheme does not operate in such bands – you need to calculate the costs precisely. Thus the fixed costs on a settlement of £2,683.00 are calculated as follows:–

Core fee	£800.00
Variable element (contingency fee) 20% of £2,683.00	536.60
	£1,336.60

As the variable element of the fee is a contingency fee – a percentage of damages – and as the maximum level of the contingency fee is 20% of damages (20% up to £5,000 damages and 15% on the balance of damages) then by using this ready reckoner you can see at a glance to within £10 of the correct costs figure.

Thus with the above damages award of £2,683.00 one looks at £2,700.00, which is the nearest round sum and reads off the fixed costs figure, which is £1,340 – that is just £3.40 out. Not bad eh?

A conditional fee success fee of 12.5% has been fixed for unissued cases (Paragraph 9 of the Civil Procedure (Amendment No. 5) Rules 2003 (see below)) and so I have calculated the amount inclusive of a 12.5% success fee. (Table 2). This came into operation on 1st March 2004. (See Chapter 3: Fixed Costs and Conditional Fees.)

20% remains the success fee for fixed-costs cases taken on between 6th October 2003 and 29th February 2004, inclusive (see *Callery* v *Gray* [2002] 2 Costs LR 205 (HL)) and so I have carried out a similar exercise on the basis of a 20% success fee (Table 3).

In and around London there is a 12.5% "London weighting" allowance. (Rule 45.9(2) CPR). Table 4 gives the fixed costs figure for the "golden ring" area, which is of course the same calculation as for a 12.5% success fee in a standard fee case.

Matters become more complicated when you add a 12.5% success fee to the golden ring rate. The 12.5% fixed success fee is calculated on the *ordinary* rate *not* the enhanced rate. Thus the overall enhancement is 25% being a 12.5% enhancement at a 12.5% success fee on 100% *not* on 112.5%. This is achieved by Paragraph 9 of the Civil Procedure (Amendment No. 5) Rules 2003 (Statutory Instrument 2003 No. 3361 (L38)):

> "(2)The amount of the success fee shall be 12.5% of the fixed recoverable costs calculated in accordance with rule 45.9(1), *disregarding* (my emphasis) any additional amount which may be included in the fixed recoverable costs by virtue of rule 45.9(2)."
>
> 45.9(2) is the 12.5% enhancement for London-based firms. Thus the 12.5% success fee is based on the *ordinary* rates and not the enhanced rates.

Table 5 gives these figures.

If you are in the golden ring area *and* you are feeling lucky, go for the 20% success fee on your 112.5% in relation to cases taken on between 6th October 2003 and 29th February 2004 inclusive. Again I have made the calculations for you. (Table 6)

Thus the Ready Reckoners are as follows:

Table 1.   Standard Rate – no success fee

Table 2.   Standard Rate – 12.5% success fee

Table 3.   Standard Rate – 20% success fee

Table 4.   Enhanced Rate – no success fee

Table 5.   Enhanced Rate – 12.5% success fee

Table 6.   Enhanced Rate – 20% success fee

I have also carried out the VAT calculation in each case as fixed costs attract VAT which is payable by the other side. In other words the fixed costs figures in the rules and regulations etc. are *exclusive* of VAT.

Ready Reckoners: Table 1

Standard Rate – no success fee

Damages	Fixed Costs	VAT thereon	Total (Excluding disbursements)
1,000	1,000.00	175.00	1,175.00
1,100	1,020.00	178.50	1,198.50
1,200	1,040.00	182.00	1,222.00
1,300	1,060.00	185.50	1,245.50
1,400	1,080.00	189.00	1,269.00
1,500	1,100.00	192.50	1,292.50
1,600	1,120.00	196.00	1,316.00
1,700	1,140.00	199.50	1,339.50
1,800	1,160.00	203.00	1,363.00
1,900	1,180.00	206.50	1,386.50
2,000	1,200.00	210.00	1,410.00
2,100	1,220.00	213.50	1,433.50
2,200	1,240.00	217.00	1,457.00
2,300	1,260.00	220.50	1,480.50
2,400	1,280.00	224.00	1,504.00
2,500	1,300.00	227.50	1,527.50

Damages	Fixed Costs	VAT thereon	Total (Excluding disbursements)
2,600	1,320.00	231.00	1,551.00
2,700	1,340.00	234.50	1,574.50
2,800	1,360.00	238.00	1,598.00
2,900	1,380.00	241.50	1,621.50
3,000	1,400.00	245.00	1,645.00
3,100	1,420.00	248.50	1,668.50
3,200	1,440.00	252.00	1,692.00
3,300	1,460.00	255.50	1,715.50
3,400	1,480.00	259.00	1,739.00
3,500	1,500.00	262.50	1,762.50
3,600	1,520.00	266.00	1,786.00
3,700	1,540.00	269.50	1,809.50
3,800	1,560.00	273.00	1,833.00
3,900	1,580.00	276.50	1,856.50
4,000	1,600.00	280.00	1,880.00
4,100	1,620.00	283.50	1,903.50
4,200	1,640.00	287.00	1,927.00
4,300	1,660.00	290.50	1,950.50

Damages	Fixed Costs	VAT thereon	Total (Excluding disbursements)
4,400	1,680.00	294.00	1,974.00
4,500	1,700.00	297.50	1,997.50
4,600	1,720.00	301.00	2,021.00
4,700	1,740.00	304.50	2,044.50
4,800	1,760.00	308.00	2,068.00
4,900	1,780.00	311.50	2,091.50
5,000	1,800.00	315.00	2,115.00
5,100	1,815.00	317.63	2,132.63
5,200	1,830.00	320.25	2,150.25
5,300	1,845.00	322.88	2,167.88
5,400	1,860.00	325.50	2,185.50
5,500	1,875.00	328.13	2,203.13
5,600	1,890.00	330.75	2,220.75
5,700	1,905.00	333.38	2,238.38
5,800	1,920.00	336.00	2,256.00
5,900	1,935.00	338.63	2,273.63
6,000	1,950.00	341.25	2,291.25
6,100	1,965.00	343.88	2,308.88

Damages	Fixed Costs	VAT thereon	Total (Excluding disbursements)
6,200	1,980.00	346.50	2,326.50
6,300	1,995.00	349.13	2,344.13
6,400	2,010.00	351.75	2,361.75
6,500	2,025.00	354.38	2,379.38
6,600	2,040.00	357.00	2,397.00
6,700	2,055.00	359.63	2,414.63
6,800	2,070.00	362.25	2,432.25
6,900	2,085.00	364.88	2,449.88
7,000	2,100.00	367.50	2,467.50
7,100	2,115.00	370.13	2,485.13
7,200	2,130.00	372.75	2,502.75
7,300	2,145.00	375.38	2,520.38
7,400	2,160.00	378.00	2,538.00
7,500	2,175.00	380.63	2,555.63
7,600	2,190.00	383.25	2,573.25
7,700	2,205.00	385.88	2,590.88
7,800	2,220.00	388.50	2,608.50
7,900	2,235.00	391.13	2,626.13

Damages	Fixed Costs	VAT thereon	Total (Excluding disbursements)
8,000	2,250.00	393.75	2,643.75
8,100	2,265.00	396.38	2,661.38
8,200	2,280.00	399.00	2,679.00
8,300	2,295.00	401.63	2,696.63
8,400	2,310.00	404.25	2,714.25
8,500	2,325.00	406.88	2,731.88
8,600	2,340.00	409.50	2,749.50
8,700	2,355.00	412.13	2,767.13
8,800	2,370.00	414.75	2,784.75
8,900	2,385.00	417.38	2,802.38
9,000	2,400.00	420.00	2,820.00
9,100	2,415.00	422.63	2,837.63
9,200	2,430.00	425.25	2,855.25
9,300	2,445.00	427.88	2,872.88
9,400	2,460.00	430.50	2,890.50
9,500	2,475.00	433.13	2,908.13
9,600	2,490.00	435.75	2,925.75
9,700	2,505.00	438.38	2,943.38

Damages	Fixed Costs	VAT thereon	Total (Excluding disbursements)
9,800	2,520.00	441.00	2,961.00
9,900	2,535.00	443.63	2,978.63
10,000	2,550.00	446.25	2,996.25

Above £10,000 scheme does not apply.

Ready Reckoners: Table 2

Standard Rate – 12.5% success fee

Damages	Fixed Costs	VAT thereon	Total (Excluding disbursements)
1,000	1,125.00	196.88	1,321.88
1,100	1,147.50	200.81	1,348.31
1,200	1,170.00	204.75	1,374.75
1,300	1,192.50	208.69	1,401.19
1,400	1,215.00	212.63	1,427.63
1,500	1,237.50	216.56	1,454.06
1,600	1,260.00	220.50	1,480.50
1,700	1,282.50	224.44	1,506.94
1,800	1,305.00	228.38	1,533.38
1,900	1,327.50	232.31	1,559.81
2,000	1,350.00	236.25	1,586.25
2,100	1,372.50	240.19	1,612.69
2,200	1,395.00	244.13	1,639.13
2,300	1,417.50	248.06	1,665.56
2,400	1,440.00	252.00	1,692.00
2,500	1,462.50	255.94	1,718.44

Damages	Fixed Costs	VAT thereon	Total (Excluding disbursements)
2,600	1,485.00	259.88	1,744.88
2,700	1,507.50	263.81	1,771.31
2,800	1,530.00	267.75	1,797.75
2,900	1,552.50	271.69	1,824.19
3,000	1,575.00	275.63	1,850.63
3,100	1,597.50	279.56	1,877.06
3,200	1,620.00	283.50	1,903.50
3,300	1,642.50	287.44	1,929.94
3,400	1,665.00	291.38	1,956.38
3,500	1,687.50	295.31	1,982.81
3,600	1,710.00	299.25	2,009.25
3,700	1,732.50	303.19	2,035.69
3,800	1,755.00	307.13	2,062.13
3,900	1,777.50	311.06	2,088.56
4,000	1,800.00	315.00	2,115.00
4,100	1,822.50	318.94	2,141.44
4,200	1,845.00	322.88	2,167.88
4,300	1,867.50	326.81	2,194.31

Damages	Fixed Costs	VAT thereon	Total (Excluding disbursements)
4,400	1,890.00	330.75	2,220.75
4,500	1,912.50	334.69	2,247.19
4,600	1,935.00	338.63	2,273.63
4,700	1,957.50	342.56	2,300.06
4,800	1,980.00	346.50	2,326.50
4,900	2,002.50	350.44	2,352.94
5,000	2,025.00	354.38	2,379.38
5,100	2,041.88	357.33	2,399.21
5,200	2,058.75	360.28	2,419.03
5,300	2,075.63	363.24	2,438.87
5,400	2,092.50	366.19	2,458.69
5,500	2,109.38	369.14	2,478.52
5,600	2,126.25	372.09	2,498.34
5,700	2,143.13	375.05	2,518.18
5,800	2,160.00	378.00	2,538.00
5,900	2,176.88	380.95	2,557.83
6,000	2,193.75	383.91	2,577.66
6,100	2,210.63	386.86	2,597.49

Damages	Fixed Costs	VAT thereon	Total (Excluding disbursements)
6,200	2,227.50	389.81	2,617.31
6,300	2,244.38	392.77	2,637.15
6,400	2,261.25	395.72	2,656.97
6,500	2,278.13	398.67	2,676.80
6,600	2,295.00	401.63	2,696.63
6,700	2,311.88	404.58	2,716.46
6,800	2,328.75	407.53	2,736.28
6,900	2,345.63	410.49	2,756.12
7,000	2,362.50	413.44	2,775.94
7,100	2,379.38	416.39	2,795.77
7,200	2,396.25	419.34	2,815.59
7,300	2,413.13	422.30	2,835.43
7,400	2,430.00	425.25	2,855.25
7,500	2,446.88	428.20	2,875.08
7,600	2,463.75	431.16	2,894.91
7,700	2,480.63	434.11	2,914.74
7,800	2,497.50	437.06	2,934.56
7,900	2,514.38	440.02	2,954.40

Damages	Fixed Costs	VAT *thereon*	Total *(Excluding disbursements)*
8,000	2,531.25	442.97	2,974.22
8,100	2,548.13	445.92	2,994.05
8,200	2,565.00	448.88	3,013.88
8,300	2,581.88	451.83	3,033.71
8,400	2,598.75	454.78	3,053.53
8,500	2,615.63	457.74	3,073.37
8,600	2,632.50	460.69	3,093.19
8,700	2,649.38	463.64	3,113.02
8,800	2,666.25	466.59	3,132.84
8,900	2,683.13	469.55	3,152.68
9,000	2,700.00	472.50	3,172.50
9,100	2,716.88	475.45	3,192.33
9,200	2,733.75	478.41	3,212.16
9,300	2,750.63	481.36	3,231.99
9,400	2,767.50	484.31	3,251.81
9,500	2,784.38	487.27	3,271.65
9,600	2,801.25	490.22	3,291.47
9,700	2,818.13	493.17	3,311.30

Damages	Fixed Costs	VAT thereon	Total (Excluding disbursements)
9,800	2,835.00	496.13	3,331.13
9,900	2,851.88	499.08	3,350.96
10,000	2,868.75	502.03	3,370.78

Above £10,000 scheme does not apply.

Ready Reckoners: Table 3

Standard Rate – 20% success fee

(Applicable to cases taken on between 6th October 2003 and 29th February 2004 where the cause of action arose on or after 6th October 2003.)

Damages	Fixed Costs	VAT thereon	Total (Excluding disbursements)
1,000	1,200.00	210.00	1,410.00
1,100	1,224.00	214.20	1,438.20
1,200	1,248.00	218.40	1,466.40
1,300	1,272.00	222.60	1,494.60
1,400	1,296.00	226.80	1,522.80
1,500	1,320.00	231.00	1,551.00
1,600	1,344.00	235.20	1,579.20
1,700	1,368.00	239.40	1,607.40
1,800	1,392.00	243.60	1,635.60
1,900	1,416.00	247.80	1,663.80
2,000	1,440.00	252.00	1,692.00
2,100	1,464.00	256.20	1,720.20
2,200	1,488.00	260.40	1,748.40
2,300	1,512.00	264.60	1,776.60

Damages	Fixed Costs	VAT thereon	Total (Excluding disbursements)
2,400	1,536.00	268.80	1,804.80
2,500	1,560.00	273.00	1,833.00
2,600	1,584.00	277.20	1,861.20
2,700	1,608.00	281.40	1,889.40
2,800	1,632.00	285.60	1,917.60
2,900	1,656.00	289.80	1,945.80
3,000	1,680.00	294.00	1,974.00
3,100	1,704.00	298.20	2,002.20
3,200	1,728.00	302.40	2,030.40
3,300	1,752.00	306.60	2,058.60
3,400	1,776.00	310.80	2,086.80
3,500	1,800.00	315.00	2,115.00
3,600	1,824.00	319.20	2,143.20
3,700	1,848.00	323.40	2,171.40
3,800	1,872.00	327.60	2,199.60
3,900	1,896.00	331.80	2,227.80
4,000	1,920.00	336.00	2,256.00
4,100	1,944.00	340.20	2,284.20

Damages	Fixed Costs	VAT thereon	Total (Excluding disbursements)
4,200	1,968.00	344.40	2,312.40
4,300	1,992.00	348.60	2,340.60
4,400	2,016.00	352.80	2,368.80
4,500	2,040.00	357.00	2,397.00
4,600	2,064.00	361.20	2,425.20
4,700	2,088.00	365.40	2,453.40
4,800	2,112.00	369.60	2,481.60
4,900	2,136.00	373.80	2,509.80
5,000	2,160.00	378.00	2,538.00
5,100	2,178.00	381.15	2,559.15
5,200	2,196.00	384.30	2,580.30
5,300	2,214.00	387.45	2,601.45
5,400	2,232.00	390.60	2,622.60
5,500	2,250.00	393.75	2,643.75
5,600	2,268.00	396.90	2,664.90
5,700	2,286.00	400.05	2,686.05
5,800	2,304.00	403.20	2,707.20
5,900	2,322.00	406.35	2,728.35

Damages	Fixed Costs	VAT thereon	Total (Excluding disbursements)
6,000	2,340.00	409.50	2,749.50
6,100	2,358.00	412.65	2,770.65
6,200	2,376.00	415.80	2,791.80
6,300	2,394.00	418.95	2,812.95
6,400	2,412.00	422.10	2,834.10
6,500	2,430.00	425.25	2,855.25
6,600	2,448.00	428.40	2,876.40
6,700	2,466.00	431.55	2,897.55
6,800	2,484.00	434.70	2,918.70
6,900	2,502.00	437.85	2,939.85
7,000	2,520.00	441.00	2,961.00
7,100	2,538.00	444.15	2,982.15
7,200	2,556.00	447.30	3,003.30
7,300	2,574.00	450.45	3,024.45
7,400	2,592.00	453.60	3,045.60
7,500	2,610.00	456.75	3,066.75
7,600	2,628.00	459.90	3,087.90
7,700	2,646.00	463.05	3,109.05

Damages	Fixed Costs	VAT thereon	Total (Excluding disbursements)
7,800	2,664.00	466.20	3,130.20
7,900	2,682.00	469.35	3,151.35
8,000	2,700.00	472.50	3,172.50
8,100	2,718.00	475.65	3,193.65
8,200	2,736.00	478.80	3,214.80
8,300	2,754.00	481.95	3,235.95
8,400	2,772.00	485.10	3,257.10
8,500	2,790.00	488.25	3,278.25
8,600	2,808.00	491.40	3,299.40
8,700	2,826.00	494.55	3,320.55
8,800	2,844.00	497.70	3,341.70
8,900	2,862.00	500.85	3,362.85
9,000	2,880.00	504.00	3,384.00
9,100	2,898.00	507.15	3,405.15
9,200	2,916.00	510.30	3,426.30
9,300	2,934.00	513.45	3,447.45
9,400	2,952.00	516.60	3,468.60
9,500	2,970.00	519.75	3,489.75

Damages	Fixed Costs	VAT thereon	Total (Excluding disbursements)
9,600	2,988.00	522.90	3,510.90
9,700	3,006.00	526.05	3,532.05
9,800	3,024.00	529.20	3,553.20
9,900	3,042.00	532.35	3,574.35
10,000	3,060.00	535.50	3,595.50

Above £10,000 scheme does not apply.

Ready Reckoners: Table 4

Enhanced Rate – no success fee

Damages	Fixed Costs	VAT thereon	Total (Excluding disbursements)
1,000	1,125.00	196.88	1,321.88
1,100	1,147.50	200.81	1,348.31
1,200	1,170.00	204.75	1,374.75
1,300	1,192.50	208.69	1,401.19
1,400	1,215.00	212.63	1,427.63
1,500	1,237.50	216.56	1,454.06
1,600	1,260.00	220.50	1,480.50
1,700	1,282.50	224.44	1,506.94
1,800	1,305.00	228.38	1,533.38
1,900	1,327.50	232.31	1,559.81
2,000	1,350.00	236.25	1,586.25
2,100	1,372.50	240.19	1,612.69
2,200	1,395.00	244.13	1,639.13
2,300	1,417.50	248.06	1,665.56
2,400	1,440.00	252.00	1,692.00
2,500	1,462.50	255.94	1,718.44

Damages	Fixed Costs	VAT thereon	Total (Excluding disbursements)
2,600	1,485.00	259.88	1,744.88
2,700	1,507.50	263.81	1,771.31
2,800	1,530.00	267.75	1,797.75
2,900	1,552.50	271.69	1,824.19
3,000	1,575.00	275.63	1,850.63
3,100	1,597.50	279.56	1,877.06
3,200	1,620.00	283.50	1,903.50
3,300	1,642.50	287.44	1,929.94
3,400	1,665.00	291.38	1,956.38
3,500	1,687.50	295.31	1,982.81
3,600	1,710.00	299.25	2,009.25
3,700	1,732.50	303.19	2,035.69
3,800	1,755.00	307.13	2,062.13
3,900	1,777.50	311.06	2,088.56
4,000	1,800.00	315.00	2,115.00
4,100	1,822.50	318.94	2,141.44
4,200	1,845.00	322.88	2,167.88
4,300	1,867.50	326.81	2,194.31

Damages	Fixed Costs	VAT *thereon*	Total *(Excluding disbursements)*
4,400	1,890.00	330.75	2,220.75
4,500	1,912.50	334.69	2,247.19
4,600	1,935.00	338.63	2,273.63
4,700	1,957.50	342.56	2,300.06
4,800	1,980.00	346.50	2,326.50
4,900	2,002.50	350.44	2,352.94
5,000	2,025.00	354.38	2,379.38
5,100	2,041.88	357.33	2,399.21
5,200	2,058.75	360.28	2,419.03
5,300	2,075.63	363.24	2,438.87
5,400	2,092.50	366.19	2,458.69
5,500	2,109.38	369.14	2,478.52
5,600	2,126.25	372.09	2,498.34
5,700	2,143.13	375.05	2,518.18
5,800	2,160.00	378.00	2,538.00
5,900	2,176.88	380.95	2,557.83
6,000	2,193.75	383.91	2,577.66
6,100	2,210.63	386.86	2,597.49

Damages	Fixed Costs	VAT thereon	Total (Excluding disbursements)
6,200	2,227.50	389.81	2,617.31
6,300	2,244.38	392.77	2,637.15
6,400	2,261.25	395.72	2,656.97
6,500	2,278.13	398.67	2,676.80
6,600	2,295.00	401.63	2,696.63
6,700	2,311.88	404.58	2,716.46
6,800	2,328.75	407.53	2,736.28
6,900	2,345.63	410.49	2,756.12
7,000	2,362.50	413.44	2,775.94
7,100	2,379.38	416.39	2,795.77
7,200	2,396.25	419.34	2,815.59
7,300	2,413.13	422.30	2,835.43
7,400	2,430.00	425.25	2,855.25
7,500	2,446.88	428.20	2,875.08
7,600	2,463.75	431.16	2,894.91
7,700	2,480.63	434.11	2,914.74
7,800	2,497.50	437.06	2,934.56
7,900	2,514.38	440.02	2,954.40

Damages	Fixed Costs	VAT thereon	Total (Excluding disbursements)
8,000	2,531.25	442.97	2,974.22
8,100	2,548.13	445.92	2,994.05
8,200	2,565.00	448.88	3,013.88
8,300	2,581.88	451.83	3,033.71
8,400	2,598.75	454.78	3,053.53
8,500	2,615.63	457.74	3,073.37
8,600	2,632.50	460.69	3,093.19
8,700	2,649.38	463.64	3,113.02
8,800	2,666.25	466.59	3,132.84
8,900	2,683.13	469.55	3,152.68
9,000	2,700.00	472.50	3,172.50
9,100	2,716.88	475.45	3,192.33
9,200	2,733.75	478.41	3,212.16
9,300	2,750.63	481.36	3,231.99
9,400	2,767.50	484.31	3,251.81
9,500	2,784.38	487.27	3,271.65
9,600	2,801.25	490.22	3,291.47
9,700	2,818.13	493.17	3,311.30

Damages	Fixed Costs	VAT thereon	Total (Excluding disbursements)
9,800	2,835.00	496.13	3,331.13
9,900	2,851.88	499.08	3,350.96
10,000	2,868.75	502.03	3,370.78

Above £10,000 scheme does not apply.

Ready Reckoners: Table 5

Enhanced Rate – 12.5% success fee

Damages	Fixed Costs	VAT *thereon*	Total *(Excluding disbursements)*
1,000	1,250.00	218.75	1,468.75
1,100	1,275.00	223.13	1,498.13
1,200	1,300.00	227.50	1,527.50
1,300	1,325.00	231.88	1,556.88
1,400	1,350.00	236.25	1,586.25
1,500	1,375.00	240.63	1,615.63
1,600	1,400.00	245.00	1,645.00
1,700	1,425.00	249.38	1,674.38
1,800	1,450.00	253.75	1,703.75
1,900	1,475.00	258.13	1,733.13
2,000	1,500.00	262.50	1,762.50
2,100	1,525.00	266.88	1,791.88
2,200	1,550.00	271.25	1,821.25
2,300	1,575.00	275.63	1,850.63
2,400	1,600.00	280.00	1,880.00
2,500	1,625.00	284.38	1,909.38

Damages	Fixed Costs	VAT thereon	Total (Excluding disbursements)
2,600	1,650.00	288.75	1,938.75
2,700	1,675.00	293.13	1,968.13
2,800	1,700.00	297.50	1,997.50
2,900	1,725.00	301.88	2,026.88
3,000	1,750.00	306.25	2,056.25
3,100	1,775.00	310.63	2,085.63
3,200	1,800.00	315.00	2,115.00
3,300	1,825.00	319.38	2,144.38
3,400	1,850.00	323.75	2,173.75
3,500	1,875.00	328.13	2,203.13
3,600	1,900.00	332.50	2,232.50
3,700	1,925.00	336.88	2,261.88
3,800	1,950.00	341.25	2,291.25
3,900	1,975.00	345.63	2,320.63
4,000	2,000.00	350.00	2,350.00
4,100	2,025.00	354.38	2,379.38
4,200	2,050.00	358.75	2,408.75
4,300	2,075.00	363.13	2,438.13

Damages	Fixed Costs	VAT thereon	Total (Excluding disbursements)
4,400	2,100.00	367.50	2,467.50
4,500	2,125.00	371.88	2,496.88
4,600	2,150.00	376.25	2,526.25
4,700	2,175.00	380.63	2,555.63
4,800	2,200.00	385.00	2,585.00
4,900	2,225.00	389.38	2,614.38
5,000	2,250.00	393.75	2,643.75
5,100	2,268.75	397.03	2,665.78
5,200	2,287.50	400.31	2,687.81
5,300	2,306.25	403.59	2,709.84
5,400	2,325.00	406.88	2,731.88
5,500	2,343.75	410.16	2,753.91
5,600	2,362.50	413.44	2,775.94
5,700	2,381.25	416.72	2,797.97
5,800	2,400.00	420.00	2,820.00
5,900	2,418.75	423.28	2,842.03
6,000	2,437.50	426.56	2,864.06
6,100	2,456.25	429.84	2,886.09

Damages	Fixed Costs	VAT thereon	Total (Excluding disbursements)
6,200	2,475.00	433.13	2,908.13
6,300	2,493.75	436.41	2,930.16
6,400	2,512.50	439.69	2,952.19
6,500	2,531.25	442.97	2,974.22
6,600	2,550.00	446.25	2,996.25
6,700	2,568.75	449.53	3,018.28
6,800	2,587.50	452.81	3,040.31
6,900	2,606.25	456.09	3,062.34
7,000	2,625.00	459.38	3,084.38
7,100	2,643.75	462.66	3,106.41
7,200	2,662.50	465.94	3,128.44
7,300	2,681.25	469.22	3,150.47
7,400	2,700.00	472.50	3,172.50
7,500	2,718.75	475.78	3,194.53
7,600	2,737.50	479.06	3,216.56
7,700	2,756.25	482.34	3,238.59
7,800	2,775.00	485.63	3,260.63
7,900	2,793.75	488.91	3,282.66

Damages	Fixed Costs	VAT thereon	Total (Excluding disbursements)
8,000	2,812.50	492.19	3,304.69
8,100	2,831.25	495.47	3,326.72
8,200	2,850.00	498.75	3,348.75
8,300	2,868.75	502.03	3,370.78
8,400	2,887.50	505.31	3,392.81
8,500	2,906.25	508.59	3,414.84
8,600	2,925.00	511.88	3,436.88
8,700	2,943.75	515.16	3,458.91
8,800	2,962.50	518.44	3,480.94
8,900	2,981.25	521.72	3,502.97
9,000	3,000.00	525.00	3,525.00
9,100	3,018.75	528.28	3,547.03
9,200	3,037.50	531.56	3,569.06
9,300	3,056.25	534.84	3,591.09
9,400	3,075.00	538.13	3,613.13
9,500	3,093.75	541.41	3,635.16
9,600	3,112.50	544.69	3,657.19
9,700	3,131.25	547.97	3,679.22

Damages	Fixed Costs	VAT *thereon*	Total *(Excluding disbursements)*
9,800	3,150.00	551.25	3,701.25
9,900	3,168.75	554.53	3,723.28
10,000	3,187.50	557.81	3,745.31

Above £10,000 scheme does not apply.

Ready Reckoners: Table 6

Enhanced Rate – 20% success fee

(Applicable to cases taken on between 6th October 2003 and 29th February 2004 where the cause of action arose on or after 6th October 2003.)

Damages	Fixed Costs	VAT *thereon*	Total *(Excluding disbursements)*
1,000	1,350.00	236.25	1,586.25
1,100	1,377.00	240.98	1,617.98
1,200	1,404.00	245.70	1,649.70
1,300	1,431.00	250.43	1,681.43
1,400	1,458.00	255.15	1,713.15
1,500	1,485.00	259.88	1,744.88
1,600	1,512.00	264.60	1,776.60
1,700	1,539.00	269.33	1,808.33
1,800	1,566.00	274.05	1,840.05
1,900	1,593.00	278.78	1,871.78
2,000	1,620.00	283.50	1,903.50
2,100	1,647.00	288.23	1,935.23
2,200	1,674.00	292.95	1,966.95
2,300	1,701.00	297.68	1,998.68

Damages	Fixed Costs	VAT thereon	Total (Excluding disbursements)
2,400	1,728.00	302.40	2,030.40
2,500	1,755.00	307.13	2,062.13
2,600	1,782.00	311.85	2,093.85
2,700	1,809.00	316.58	2,125.58
2,800	1,836.00	321.30	2,157.30
2,900	1,863.00	326.03	2,189.03
3,000	1,890.00	330.75	2,220.75
3,100	1,917.00	335.48	2,252.48
3,200	1,944.00	340.20	2,284.20
3,300	1,971.00	344.93	2,315.93
3,400	1,998.00	349.65	2,347.65
3,500	2,025.00	354.38	2,379.38
3,600	2,052.00	359.10	2,411.10
3,700	2,079.00	363.83	2,442.83
3,800	2,106.00	368.55	2,474.55
3,900	2,133.00	373.28	2,506.28
4,000	2,160.00	378.00	2,538.00
4,100	2,187.00	382.73	2,569.73

Damages	Fixed Costs	VAT thereon	Total (Excluding disbursements)
4,200	2,214.00	387.45	2,601.45
4,300	2,241.00	392.18	2,633.18
4,400	2,268.00	396.90	2,664.90
4,500	2,295.00	401.63	2,696.63
4,600	2,322.00	406.35	2,728.35
4,700	2,349.00	411.08	2,760.08
4,800	2,376.00	415.80	2,791.80
4,900	2,403.00	420.53	2,823.53
5,000	2,430.00	425.25	2,855.25
5,100	2,450.26	428.80	2,879.06
5,200	2,470.50	432.34	2,902.84
5,300	2,490.76	435.88	2,926.64
5,400	2,511.00	439.43	2,950.43
5,500	2,531.26	442.97	2,974.23
5,600	2,551.50	446.51	2,998.01
5,700	2,571.76	450.06	3,021.82
5,800	2,592.00	453.60	3,045.60
5,900	2,612.26	457.15	3,069.41

Damages	Fixed Costs	VAT *thereon*	Total *(Excluding disbursements)*
6,000	2,632.50	460.69	3,093.19
6,100	2,652.76	464.23	3,116.99
6,200	2,673.00	467.78	3,140.78
6,300	2,693.26	471.32	3,164.58
6,400	2,713.50	474.86	3,188.36
6,500	2,733.76	478.41	3,212.17
6,600	2,754.00	481.95	3,235.95
6,700	2,774.26	485.50	3,259.76
6,800	2,794.50	489.04	3,283.54
6,900	2,814.76	492.58	3,307.34
7,000	2,835.00	496.13	3,331.13
7,100	2,855.26	499.67	3,354.93
7,200	2,875.50	503.21	3,378.71
7,300	2,895.76	506.76	3,402.52
7,400	2,916.00	510.30	3,426.30
7,500	2,936.26	513.85	3,450.11
7,600	2,956.50	517.39	3,473.89
7,700	2,976.76	520.93	3,497.69

Damages	Fixed Costs	VAT thereon	Total (Excluding disbursements)
7,800	2,997.00	524.48	3,521.48
7,900	3,017.26	528.02	3,545.28
8,000	3,037.50	531.56	3,569.06
8,100	3,057.76	535.11	3,592.87
8,200	3,078.00	538.65	3,616.65
8,300	3,098.26	542.20	3,640.46
8,400	3,118.50	545.74	3,664.24
8,500	3,138.76	549.28	3,688.04
8,600	3,159.00	552.83	3,711.83
8,700	3,179.26	556.37	3,735.63
8,800	3,199.50	559.91	3,759.41
8,900	3,219.76	563.46	3,783.22
9,000	3,240.00	567.00	3,807.00
9,100	3,260.26	570.55	3,830.81
9,200	3,280.50	574.09	3,854.59
9,300	3,300.76	577.63	3,878.39
9,400	3,321.00	581.18	3,902.18
9,500	3,341.26	584.72	3,925.98

Damages	Fixed Costs	VAT thereon	Total (Excluding disbursements)
9,600	3,361.50	588.26	3,949.76
9,700	3,381.76	591.81	3,973.57
9,800	3,402.00	595.35	3,997.35
9,900	3,422.26	598.90	4,021.16
10,000	3,442.50	602.44	4,044.94

Above £10,000 scheme does not apply.

CHAPTER 5
DISBURSEMENTS

CHAPTER 5
DISBURSEMENTS

Part 45.10 of the Civil Procedure Rules reads:

Disbursements

45.10 (1) The court –

(a) may allow a claim for a disbursement of a type mentioned in paragraph (2); but

(b) must not allow a claim for any other type of disbursement.

(2) The disbursements referred to in paragraph (1) are –

(a) the cost of obtaining –

(i) medical records;

(ii) a medical report;

(iii) a police report;

(iv) an engineer's report; or

(v) a search of the records of the Driver Vehicle Licensing Authority;

(b) the amount of an insurance premium; or, where a body of a prescribed description within the meaning of section 30(1) of the Access to Justice Act 1999 undertakes to meet liabilities incurred to pay the costs of other parties to proceedings, a sum not exceeding such additional amount of costs as would be allowed under section 30 in respect of provision made against the risk of having to meet such liabilities;

(c) where they are necessarily incurred by reason of one or more of the claimants being a child or patient as defined Part 21 –

(i) fees payable for instructing counsel; or

(ii) court fees payable on an application to the court.

(d) any other disbursement that has arisen due to a particular feature of the dispute.

("insurance premium" is defined in rule 43.2).

That part of Rule 45.10(2)(b) dealing with the notional premium is new, having been inserted by the Civil Procedure (Amendment No 5) Rules 2003, the explanatory note to which reads: "Rule 45.10 is amended to clarify that, in costs-only proceedings brought under Section II of Part 45 by a party funded by a body which indemnifies its members or other persons against liabilities for costs which they may incur in proceedings, the court may allow that party as a disbursement a sum not exceeding such amount as would be allowed under section 30 of the Access to Justice Act 1999."

This also raises the interesting question of whether a sum received as a notional premium is subject to income tax. Clearly if an actual premium had been incurred and recovered there would be no tax payable. Why should it be any different for a notional premium, especially when the rule and the explanatory note refer to it as a "disbursement"?

For firms doing Membership Organisation work notional premia add up and the tax or lack of it will be a very substantial sum.

My view is that it is taxable income and is wrongly described as a disbursement. Rather it is an enhancement of the solicitor's fee for taking extra risk.

Disputes as to disbursements

Practice Direction 25A.10 provides:

If the parties agree the amount of the fixed recoverable costs and the only dispute is as to the payment of, or amount of, a disbursement or as to the amount of a success fee, then proceedings should be issued under rule 44.12A in the normal way and not by reference to Section II of Part 45.

If costs only proceedings are commenced using the procedure set out in rule 44.12A then a claim form must be issued in accordance with Part 8 of the Civil Procedure Rules.

Practice Direction 25A.9 states:

> The claimant must also include on the claim form details of any disbursements or success fee he wishes to claim. The disbursements that may be claimed are set out in rule 45.10(1). If the disbursement falls within 45.10(2)(d) (disbursements that have arisen due to a particular feature of the dispute) the claimant must give details of the exceptional feature of the dispute and why he considers the disbursement to be necessary.

Thus costs are fixed but disbursements are not and this is a major flaw of the new scheme – that there is still scope for argument about our old friend the recoverable after-the-event insurance premium – as well as more tangible disbursements.

While there can be no argument about fixed costs there can be arguments in relation to disbursements both as to the amount of the disbursement and as to whether it was reasonable to incur it at all.

Thus although an engineer's report is a potentially allowable disbursement it may be difficult to justify commissioning such a report in a low-value road traffic accident claim where liability is not contested. Disputes about disbursements, particularly experts' reports, are likely to become more common as the fixed costs regime is extended to employers' liability areas and public liability cases, probably in 2005.

The other disbursements listed in 45.10(2), namely medical records, *a* medical report (note the singular), a police report and a DVLA search should cause no significant problem.

After-the-event Insurance

"The amount of an insurance premium" referred to in 45.10(2)(b) is of course the recoverable after-the-event insurance premium and clearly there is scope for argument as to whether such a disbursement is necessary and, if so, what the correct level of premium should be.

The very fact that a rule dealing with just recoverable fixed costs cases specifically allows the court to allow recovery of an after-the-event insurance premium would appear to demonstrate that, in principle, such a disbursement is recoverable even though one might query the need for it in a case where costs are both fixed and relatively low.

The claimant argument is that one needs after-the-event insurance in every case because you never know which case is going to be defended, whether it be on liability or quantum and to only insure cases that are issued makes the premium unaffordably expensive.

The arguments for and against after-the-event insurance premia in fixed recoverable costs cases are no different from those in *Callery* v *Gray* – a classic fixed costs case.

Thus I have no doubt that the courts will continue to allow recoverability of an after-the-event insurance premium. However *Callery* v *Gray* left open the possibility of the courts revisiting the level of premium and I believe that the amount allowed may now drop below *Callery* v *Gray* levels.

After all the overall risk is now much lower as fixed recoverable costs will eliminate, in most cases, the risk of a one-off high liability.

Clearly the answer is to fix disbursements as well and let the devil take the hindmost. A fixed disbursement allowance of, say, £500, would allow those claimant solicitors who want to insure to do so and would give significant extra profit to those claimant solicitors prepared to take a risk themselves. Risk-aversion is destroying the human race let alone the legal profession so significant reward for risk-taking is to be encouraged.

£500 would save the liability insurers some money, introduce certainty, avoid disbursement-only assessments, and allow lawyers to keep the money in the legal profession rather than passing it out to after-the-event insurers in respect of unnecessary insurance.

It would also help drive out the claims farmers still existing and masquerading as after-the-event insurers.

Counsel's Fees

Significantly counsel's fees are not recoverable as a disbursement unless the claimant is a child or patient and even then there is a requirement that they are "necessarily incurred" (45.10(2)(c)).

Quite simply if you instruct counsel then counsel's fees come out of your fixed fee. Every penny paid to counsel is a penny less for the solicitor's firm.

The choice is yours.

Clearly counsel's fees incurred in relation to an infant approval originating summons are potentially recoverable (45.10(2)(c)) as are court fees in relation to such summonses.

Curiously, and presumably because of a drafting error, there is no *additional* fee, over and above normal fixed recoverable costs, payable to a solicitor conducting an infant approval originating summons and nor are solicitor agent's fees recoverable as a disbursement in such cases.

This needs to be remedied. Again there is no reason why this sum should not be fixed at an additional fee of, say,

£350.00 plus VAT whether it be counsel, solicitor's agent or the solicitor him or herself carrying out the advocacy.

The *success fee* on counsel's fees, where counsel is acting on a conditional fee basis *is* to be fixed in road traffic accident cases *whatever their value* – see Chapter 3: Fixed Costs and Conditional Fees.

General

Whilst 45.10(1)(b) appears quite tough:

The court –

(b) must not allow a claim for any other type of disbursement"

(other than those mentioned in (2)) it is somewhat softened by the inclusion in (2) of paragraph (d)

any other disbursement that has arisen due to a particular feature of the dispute.

Travel and Subsistence etc.

The cost of travelling, for example to see a client or visit the *locus in quo*, comes out of the fixed fee.

Court Fees

The only court fees recoverable are those payable on an application to the court necessarily incurred *by reason of one or more of the claimants* being a *child or patient*. Thus on the face of it a fee for an application for pre-action disclosure is not covered.

However this is likely to be covered by the catch-all
45.10(2)(d) – "any other disbursement that has arisen due
to a particular feature of the dispute".

CHAPTER 6
THE MOTOR INSURERS' BUREAU
CONTINGENCY FEE SCHEME

CHAPTER 6
THE MOTOR INSURERS' BUREAU
CONTINGENCY FEE SCHEME

A new Motor Insurers' Bureau scheme in relation to compensation of victims of untraced drivers was agreed between the Bureau and the Secretary of State for Transport on 7 February 2003 and came into force on 14 February 2003. It applies to claims arising on or after 14 February 2003.

The new scheme introduces compensation for damage to property caused by an untraced driver and also increases significantly the legal costs payable by the bureau to applicants' solicitors.

Strikingly the system of costs is an out-and-out recoverable contingency fee scheme which I look at in detail below, after having considered the changes to the actual scheme itself.

The Scheme

The Motor Insurers' Bureau was established in 1946 and administers the guarantee fund through two agreements between the bureau and the Secretary of State for Transport.

The uninsured driver's agreement compensates those involved in accidents where the other party is uninsured. The untraced driver's agreement also compensates those involved in hit-and-run cases.

The new agreement offers an additional level of protection to the public as the untraced driver's agreement has now been brought into line with the uninsured driver's agreement so that claims may be made in relation to damage to property and not just for damages for personal injury. Such claims may include car-hire charges as well as the cost of repairs or the write-off value of the vehicle. Thus the somewhat controversial area of credit hire is now included in the untraced driver's agreement. Previously it was not as the scheme did not cover damage to property or loss flowing from such damage.

A £300 excess applies in relation to property damage only.

This change opens the system to abuse. Any self-inflicted prang in your new car could be blamed on an anonymous lorry driver and his anonymous lorry.

To avoid this potential abuse clauses 5(1)(a) and 5(3) combine to exclude payment in respect of property where there is not an identified vehicle as opposed to an identified driver. Thus it is an untraced driver scheme not an untraced vehicle scheme. (Clause 5(1)(a)).

Thus there must be proof that a qualifying incident has taken place. For example in the event of an accident involving a stolen vehicle abandoned by the thief the *vehicle* will be identified although the driver's identity will not be ascertained.

If a claim for compensation in respect of death or bodily injury is being made together with a property claim and there is no identified vehicle then only the personal injury claim, and not the property claim, will be covered by the Agreement. (Clause 5(3)).

Injury claims must be made no later than three years after the incident (Clause 4(3)(a)(i)) whether or not damage to property has also arisen from the same event but *damage to property* claims must be brought no later than *nine months* after the date of the event, whether or not death or bodily injury has also arisen from the same event. (Clause 4(3)(a)(ii)).

Thus in a claim for damages for personal injury and for damage to property there is a nine month time limit for the property element of the claim but a three year time limit for the personal injury element.

In a case where the applicant could not reasonably have been expected to have become aware of the existence of bodily injury or damage to property the application must be made as soon as practicable after s/he did become, or ought reasonably to have become, aware of it but *in any case* not later than

– fifteen years after the event in relation to the personal injury element of the claim (Clause 4(3)(b)(i));

– two years after the event in relation to the property element of the claim (Clause 4(3)(b)(ii)).

Thus there are four different time limits:

	Knowledge	**No Knowledge**
Property	9 months	2 years
Personal Injury or Death	3 years	15 years

The key thing to note is that in a mixed claim, as most claims will be, the property element *must* be brought within the relevant, shorter, time limit. The fact that there will be a personal injury claim as well does not justify bringing the property element after the nine-month limitation period.

Although this extension to the scheme is welcome it has been made unnecessarily complicated. A single three-year limitation period for all property claims, whatever the date of knowledge, and a three-year limitation period for personal injury claims, subject to the 15-year period in the case of lack of knowledge, would have been simpler.

The applicant would still need to prove that a qualifying incident has taken place and identify the other vehicle and so issues of evidence not being fresh etc. would rebound against the tardy applicant.

In any event there are very strict requirements in relation to reporting the event to the police. Again, unfortunately, there are different time limits in relation to the two types of claim. Property claims must be reported to the police within five days (Clause 4(3)(c)(ii)) and personal injury claims within fourteen days (Clause 4(3)(c)(i)).

Again if the claim involves damage to both property and person the shorter time limit, five days, applies in relation to the property element. Where it is not "reasonably possible" to report the event in time then it must be reported "as soon as reasonably possible" (Clause 4(3)(c)). The applicant must produce satisfactory evidence of having reported the matter to the police in the form of an acknowledgment from the relevant force showing the crime or incident number under which that force has recorded the matter (Clause 4(3)(d)), and must have co-operated with the police in any investigation into the event (Clause 4(3)(e)).

As we have seen there are different time limits in respect of property matters and personal injury matters and the agreement makes it clear that two separate applications may be made in respect of the same event.

Clause 4(4) reads:

> Where both death or bodily injury and damage to property have arisen from a single event nothing contained in this clause shall require an applicant to make an application in respect of the death or bodily injury on the same occasion as an application in respect of the damage to property and where two applications are made in respect of one event the provisions of this Agreement shall apply separately to each of them.

Two applications. Two fees. See below.

The usual exclusions apply to an applicant who is being carried in a vehicle that he knew was stolen or unlawfully taken (Clause 5(1)(c)(i)), not insured (5(1)(c)(ii)), being used in the course or furtherance of a crime (5(1)(c)(iii)) or being used as a means of escape from or avoidance of lawful apprehension (5(1)(c)(iv)).

There is Crown immunity (5(1)(b)) and acts of terrorism are excluded (5(1)(d)), and so are claims where the applicant's vehicle was uninsured in so far as the claim relates to damage to that vehicle (5(1)(f)) and claims which have been met in full by the applicant's own insurers (5(1)(e)).

There is a cap of £250,000 in respect of damage to property arising out of any one event, whatever the number of applicants. Thus the cap is £250,000 per *event* not per applicant (Clause 8(3)(c)).

There is power to make an interim award (7(5)(a)) or a provisional award (17(3)) or a structured settlement award (17(2)). The consequences flowing from such awards are the same as in non-MIB personal injury cases.

Costs

Fixed costs are nothing new to those dealing with the untraced driver's scheme. Under the 1996 scheme, which remains in force for events occurring before 14 February 2003, a fixed payment of £150 plus VAT was paid in respect of profit costs.

Clause 10 of the new scheme deals with the right to costs:

Contribution towards legal costs

10. (1) MIB shall, in a case where it has decided to make a compensation payment under clause 8, also include in the award a sum by way of contribution towards the cost of obtaining legal advice from a Solicitor, Barrister or Advocate in respect of –

(a) the making of an application under this Agreement;

(b) the correctness of a decision made by MIB under this Agreement; or

(c) the adequacy of an award (or a part thereof) offered by MIB under this Agreement;

that sum to be determined in accordance with the schedule to this Agreement.

(2) MIB shall not be under a duty to make a payment under paragraph (1) unless it is satisfied that the applicant did obtain legal advice in respect of any one or more of the matters specified in that paragraph.

The Schedule to the Agreement sets out the level of these costs and it will be seen that instead of a fixed payment of £150 plus VAT there is now a fee of £500 plus VAT or 15%

of the award, whichever is greater and with a cap of £3,000 plus VAT on awards of between £20,000 and £150,000.

For awards over £150,000 there is a 2% contingency fee on the whole sum, thus preserving the £3,000 gained as soon as the award hit £20,000, but allowing for a little more on very large awards. Thus the fee is static at £3,000 for awards between £20,000 and £150,000 but an award of say £250,000 would attract a £5,000 fee (2% of £250,000).

This is highly significant as such a scheme is likely to be introduced for all personal injury work of all kinds – that is a recoverable contingency fee with a minimum figure payable to ensure that relatively low value cases will be worth taking on.

The percentage contingency fee should be much higher than the 15% figure in the MIB agreement, as the whole justification for low applicants' costs in such claims is that the MIB is bound to undertake most of the work: Clause 7(1) *"MIB shall, at its own cost, take all reasonable steps to investigate the claim ..."*.

The 15% recoverable contingency fee in this scheme attracts VAT, that is it is VAT exclusive and equates to a VAT inclusive rate of 17.625%.

There is no requirement that a minimum amount of work be done. All that is required is that the legal representative has advised on the making of an application or advised on the correctness of a decision made by the MIB or on its adequacy (Clause 10(1)). In this regard it is similar to the compromise agreement system used in employment cases, something also being proposed for employer's liability cases – see Chapter 8 The Future.

It is unclear whether the indemnity principle applies but it is safer to assume that it does and to create a primary liability on the client to pay costs at least equivalent to the fixed fee and disbursements. In any event as a matter of pure law costs belong to the client and thus if a solicitor agrees to charge the client a flat fee of say £750.00 costs but recovers £1,000 costs under the scheme then the surplus £250 belongs to the client.

Play safe – make the client liable.

There is no restriction on charging the client solicitor and client costs over and above the fixed fee provided the appropriate Practice Rule 15 letter has been written and makes it clear that this will happen.

Other Points to Note

Global Offers

MIB may make a global offer to include damages, interest and costs but the matter can only be settled on this basis with the applicant's consent. (Clause 3.6 of the Schedule).

Accelerated Procedures

For those cases which do not involve great complexity or a conflict of evidence, the Agreement provides for an accelerated settlement procedure, provided both parties agree (Clause 3.7 of the Schedule and Clauses 26 and 27 of the main agreement).

Disbursements

Disbursements will be paid if they are incurred with the agreement of the MIB but counsel's fees will not be paid unless the applicant is a minor or under a disability.

Counsel's Fees

Not payable unless the applicant is a minor or under a disability. This is the same principle as in the scheme of fixed costs for ordinary, non MIB, cases.

Appeals (Oral Hearings)

Although the MIB will pay the arbitrator's fee for conducting an oral hearing the arbitrator may, in a case where it appears to him or her that there were no reasonable grounds for making the appeal, order the applicant or the applicant's solicitor to reimburse MIB the fee. (Clause 24(2)).

Where there is an oral hearing and the applicant secures an award of compensation greater than that previously offered, then, unless the arbitrator orders otherwise, MIB shall make a contribution of £500 per half day towards the cost incurred by the applicant in respect of representation by a Solicitor, Barrister or Advocate. (Clause 24(4)).

Where an oral hearing has taken place at the request of an applicant and the arbitrator is satisfied that it was unnecessary and that the matter could have been decided on the basis of written submissions he shall take that into account when making an order under Clause 23(1)(e). (Clause 23(4)).

Clause 23(1)(e) provides that subject to Clause 24 (see above) the arbitrator may order that the costs of the proceedings shall be paid by one party or allocated between the parties in such proportions as he thinks fit.

This power is not subject to any financial limit.

I set out below the relevant part of the Schedule dealing with costs. There is clearly an error in Clause 2(c) which should presumably read:–

(c) *the fee payable* where the applicant has opted for an oral hearing under clause 28.

SCHEDULE

MIB's CONTRIBUTION TOWARDS APPLICANT'S LEGAL COSTS

1. Subject to paragraph 4, MIB shall pay a contribution towards the applicant's costs of obtaining legal advice determined in accordance with paragraph 2.

2. That amount shall be the aggregate of –

    (a) the fee specified in column (2) of the table below in relation to the amount of the award specified in column (1) of that table,

    (b) the amount of value added tax charged on that fee,

    (c) where the applicant has opted for an oral hearing under clause 28, and

    (d) reasonable disbursements.

Amount of the award (1)	Specified fee (2)
Not exceeding £150,000	15% of the amount of the award subject to a minimum of £500 and a maximum of £3,000
Exceeding £150,000	2% of the amount of the award

3. For the purposes of paragraph 2 –

    "amount of the award" means the aggregate of the sum awarded by way of compensation and interest under clauses 8 and 9, before deduction of any reimbursement due to be paid to the Secretary of State for Work and Pensions through the Compensation Recovery Unit (CRU) of his Department (or to any successor of that unit), but excluding the amount of any payment due in respect of benefits and hospital charges.

"reasonable disbursements" means reasonable expenditure incurred on the applicant's behalf and agreed between the applicant and MIB before it is incurred (MIB's agreement not having been unreasonably withheld) but includes Counsel's fees only where the applicant is a minor or under a legal disability.

4. The foregoing provisions of this Schedule are without prejudice to MIB's liability under the provisions of this Agreement to pay the costs of arbitration proceedings or an arbitrator's fee."

Note that the award is calculated *before* deduction of money payable to the CRU and therefore the contingency fee is calculated on the *gross* sum, but payments due in respect of benefits and hospital charges are *not* included in the gross figure.

Set out below is a Table of Costs Examples prepared by me and a comparison with the fixed costs regime in non-MIB cases.

Note that there is no "small claims" track in MIB cases, although there is a £300 excess in relation to property damage.

In ordinary non-MIB claims the small claims track runs up to £5,000 in property damage only claims and thus there will be very many cases where an applicant is better off having an untraced driver as his or her opponent as he or she will recover legal costs in circumstances where they would not be recoverable in the County Court. The small claims track for personal injury, as opposed to property damage, stops at £1,000 in the County Court.

As we have seen there are different time limits for damage to property as opposed to personal injury and it is possible to make two applications in respect of the same incident, one in respect of damage to property and one for personal injury.

If this happens then *two* sets of costs are payable. Whether or not you will be better off making two applications rather than one will depend upon the value of each aspect of the claim.

If *each* of the two aspects of the claim are above £3,333.33 (the point where the minimum fixed fee of £500 ceases to be relevant) then it makes no difference whether one or two applications are issued.

Example

Two separate applications

	Damages	*Costs*
Property damage	4,000	600.00
Personal injury	5,000	750.00
TOTAL	9,000	1,350.00

One application

	Damages	*Costs*
TOTAL	9,000	1,350.00

However if *either* aspect of the claim is within the minimum costs band then it *does* make a difference.

Example

Two separate applications

	Damages	Costs
Property damage	1,000	500.00
Personal injury	4,000	600.00
TOTAL	5,000	1,100.00

One application

	Damages	Costs
TOTAL	5,000	750.00

At best the fee doubles by issuing two separate applications. This is where each of the two elements is within the minimum costs band *and* so is the total.

Example

Two separate applications

	Damages	Costs
Property damage	1,500	500.00
Personal injury	1,500	500.00
TOTAL	3,000	1,000.00

One application

	Damages	*Costs*
TOTAL	3,000	500.00

Success Fees

My view is that success fees are not recoverable under the MIB scheme.

Examples of Costs

Award	Costs
£0–£3,333.33	£500 (minimum)
£4,000	£600
£5,000	£750
£6,000	£900
£7,000	£1,050
£8,000	£1,200
£9,000	£1,350
£10,000	£1,500
£15,000	£2,250
£20,000–£150,000	£3,000
£200,000	£4,000 (2% of total)

All figures exclude VAT and disbursements

Comparison of Costs with Fixed Costs Regime in Road Traffice Cases – Non MIB

Award/ Settlement	MIB	Fixed Costs (Injury)	Fixed Costs (No Injury)
£500	£500	–	–
£1,000	£500	£1,000	–
£2,000	£500	£1,200	–
£3,000	£500	£1,400	–
£4,000	£600	£1,600	–
£5,000	£750	£1,800	£1,800
£6,000	£900	£1,950	£1,950
£7,000	£1,050	£2,100	£2,100
£8,000	£1,200	£2,250	£2,250
£9,000	£1,350	£2,400	£2,400
£10,000	£1,500	£2,550	£2,550
£10,000 +	15% up to a maximum of £3,000	Not applicable	

CHAPTER 7
COSTS CONTROLS BY THE COURTS

CHAPTER 7
COSTS CONTROLS BY THE COURTS

Unsurprisingly no fixed cost case has yet reached a superior court but the enthusiasm of the higher courts for fixed costs is clear and there has been a number of recent cases where courts have imposed capped costs and other cases where they have expressed support for the concept of fixed costs.

Furthermore the courts, apparently unlike the solicitors who prepare them, are beginning to take seriously the costs estimates provided at allocation and listing questionnaire stages.

Throw in proportionality and the overriding objective defined in Rule 1.1 of the Civil Procedure Rules and the courts have a veritable armoury of weapons to use to impose controls on costs in litigation.

Costs Estimates

In *Leigh* v *Michelin Tyre plc* [2003] EWCA Civ 1766, [2004] 1 Costs Law Reports, Court of Appeal, 8 December 2003, a case the importance of which cannot be exaggerated, the Court of Appeal, with the Master of the Rolls as one of the judges, made it clear that costs estimates and costs capping are to play an important and increasing role in the courts' control of cases.

This is the first time the Court of Appeal has considered the effect of costs estimates.

The Court of Appeal backed their greater use while recognising a risk of an increase in satellite litigation.

It also made it clear that costs estimates are required to include estimates of the overall costs to be incurred on the assumption that the case will not settle, and not merely estimates of future costs up to some unspecified date when the case might settle (Paragraph 37).

In the introduction to the judgment, at paragraph 1, Lord Justice Dyson said:

1.   One of the principal objects of the Woolf reforms was the control of costs. The Civil Procedure Rules include a number of innovations which were designed to enable the court to limit recoverable costs and thereby further the overriding objective defined in CPR r. 1.1. One of the innovations was the requirement that parties provide costs estimates at important stages of litigation (notably the allocation and listing questionnaire stages), and the conferring on the court of the power to take the parties' estimates into account on an assessment of costs.

In this case the claimant's solicitors filed an allocation questionnaire estimating their profit costs to date at £3,000.00 plus VAT and their overall profit costs as likely to be £6,000.00 plus VAT. The estimate was never revised.

The case was settled and the claimant's solicitors lodged a bill of costs claiming £21,741.28, of which £11,744.00 was in respect of post allocation questionnaire profit costs as compared with the estimate of £3,000.00.

The district judge made no deduction to reflect the wholly inadequate estimate of future costs and the Circuit Judge declined to interfere with that decision and permission to appeal was given because there was an important point of principle as to the relevance of costs estimates in the assessment of costs.

The Court of Appeal set out the relevant Rules and Practice Directions and in particular it drew attention to Paragraphs 6.3 to 6.6 of the amended CPR 43 Practice Direction:

6.3 The court may at any stage in a case order any party to file an estimate of costs and to serve copies of the estimate on all other parties. The court may direct that the estimate be prepared in such a way as to demonstrate the likely effects of giving or not giving a particular case management direction which the court is considering, for example a direction for a split trial or for the trial of a preliminary issue. The court may specify a time limit for filing and serving the estimate. However, if no time limit is specified the estimate should be filed and served within 28 days of the date of the order.

6.4 (1) When a party to a claim which is outside the financial scope of the small claims track files an allocation questionnaire he must also file an estimate of base costs and serve a copy of it on every other party, unless the court otherwise directs. The legal representative must in addition serve an estimate upon the party he represents.

(2) Where a party to a claim which is being dealt with on the fast track or the multi track, or under Part 8, files a listing questionnaire, he must also file an estimate of base costs and serve a copy of it on every other party, unless the court otherwise directs. Where a party is represented, the legal representative must in addition serve an estimate on the party he represents.

(3) This paragraph does not apply to litigants in person.

6.5 An estimate of base costs should be substantially in the form illustrated in Precedent H in the Schedule of Costs Precedents annexed to the Practice Direction.

6.6 On an assessment of the costs of a party the court may have regard to any estimate previously filed by that party, or by any other party in the same proceedings. Such an estimate may be taken into account as a factor among others, when assessing the reasonableness of any costs claimed."

Paragraph 6.6 was at the heart of this appeal.

The Court of Appeal continued:

6. The only rule relating to the assessment of costs to which we need refer is CPR r. 44.5 which provides for the factors that are to be taken into account in deciding the amount of costs:

"(1) The court is to have regard to all the circumstances in deciding whether costs were –

(a) if it is assessing costs on the standard basis –

(i) proportionately and reasonably incurred; or

(ii) were proportionate and reasonable in amount, or

(b) if it is assessing costs on the indemnity basis –

(iii) unreasonably incurred; or

(iv) unreasonable in amount.

(2) In particular the court must give effect to any orders which have already been made.

(3) The court must also have regard to –

(a) the conduct of all the parties, including in particular –

(i) conduct before, as well as during, the proceedings; and

(ii) the efforts made, if any, before and during the proceedings in order to try to resolve the dispute;

(b) the amount or value of any money or property involved;

(c) the importance of the matter to all the parties;

(d) the particular complexity of the matter or the difficulty or novelty of the questions raised;

(e) the skill, effort, specialized knowledge and responsibility involved;

(f) the time spent on the case; and

(g) the place where and the circumstances in which work or any part of it was done.

(Rule 35.4(4) gives the court power to limit the amount that a party may recover with regard to the fees and expenses of an expert.)

7. The notes in the current edition of the White
    Book state at para. 44.7.2:

> "On completing the allocation questionnaire
> and the listing questionnaire the party must
> set out an estimate of costs incurred to date
> and an estimate of likely future costs, Section
> 6 of the Costs Practice Direction deals with
> this. Considerable care and precision is
> required in the preparation of such estimates
> since the estimates of opposing parties are
> likely to be compared one with another. An
> over-generous estimate may result in an
> opponent recovering a similar amount, while
> an under-generous estimate may result in a
> recovery on behalf of the client which does
> not reflect the actual costs involved."

The Court of Appeal went on to stress that costs estimates
are an important part of the machinery of case
management and while accepting that it will not always
be possible to provide a reasonably accurate estimate of
likely overall costs at allocation questionnaire stage "it
should usually be possible to do so even at that stage,
especially in run of the mill cases".

It also pointed out that where it becomes clear during the
course of the litigation that the estimate was inaccurate it is
all the more important to comply with the obligation in
CPR 43 Practice Direction 6.4(2) to file an up-dated estimate
at the listing questionnaire stage. (See paragraphs 16 and 17
of the judgment.)

The Court of Appeal quoted, with approval, from its own
decision in *Jefferson* v *National Freight Carriers plc* [2001]
2 Costs LR 313, itself approving Judge Alton's statement
in that case in the County Court:

> In modern litigation, with the emphasis on
> proportionality, there is a requirement for parties to

make an assessment at the outset of the likely value of the claim and its importance and complexity, and then to plan in advance the necessary work, the appropriate level of person to carry out the work, the overall time which would be necessary and appropriate [to] spend on the various stages in bringing the action to trial and the likely overall cost. While it was not unusual for costs to exceed the amount in issue, it was, in the context of modest litigation such as the present case, one reason for seeking to curb the amount of work done, and the cost by reference to the need for proportionality.

The Court of Appeal then considered the question of the legal status of the Practice Directions accompanying the Civil Procedure Rules and held that:

In our judgment, the provisions in the practice direction as to the giving of estimates of costs at various stages of the litigation are made pursuant to the power in the court to regulate its own procedure within the limits set by the statutory rules and to fill in gaps left by those rules. *(Paragraph 21.)*

It also pointed out that CPR r. 44.14 gives the court the power to disallow all or part of the costs which are being assessed where a party or his legal representative fails to comply with a rule or practice direction.

It continued:

22. The judge questioned the purpose of the provision of costs estimates. As we have said, it is to enable all parties to the litigation to know what their potential liability for costs may be. That enables them to decide whether to attempt to settle the litigation, or to pursue it, and (in the latter case) what resources to apply to the litigation. But at least as importantly, it also enables the court to take account of the likely

costs in determining what directions to give. In so far as the judge was suggesting that costs estimates are unnecessary, and will merely add to the costs of the litigation, he was wrong to do so. The practice direction is expressed in clear mandatory terms: costs estimates must be provided. It is also to be noted that it requires the legal representatives to serve the costs estimates on their clients. Apart perhaps from cases such as the present where a solicitor acts for a client who makes it clear that he or she does not require such estimates, it is also part of a solicitor's ordinary professional duty to provide the client with an estimate of future costs.

The Court of Appeal then laid down a non-exhaustive three-stage guide to applying paragraph 6.6 of the Practice Direction.

Firstly, the estimates made by solicitors of the overall likely costs of the litigation should usually provide a useful yardstick by which the reasonableness of the costs finally claimed may be measured.

If there is a substantial difference between the estimated costs and the costs claimed, that difference calls for an explanation. In the absence of a satisfactory explanation, the court may conclude that the difference itself is evidence from which it can conclude that the costs claimed are unreasonable.

Secondly, the court may take the estimated costs into account if the other party shows that it relied on the estimate in a certain way, for example by not making an offer but carrying on with the litigation on the basis that the potential liability for costs would be as per the estimate.

Thirdly, the court may take the estimate into account in cases where it decides that it would probably have given different case management directions if a realistic estimate had been given.

It gives the example of a claimant, at allocation questionnaire stage, estimating overall costs at £20,000.00 but subsequently claiming £50,000.00. The court might conclude that it would have given different directions had it know the true position. It might, for example, have trimmed the number of experts and taken other steps to slim down the complexity of the litigation in the interests of controlling costs in a reasonable and proportionate manner.

The Court of Appeal went on to say that if none of these features applied and the costs were otherwise reasonable and proportionate then it would be wrong to reduce the costs *simply* because they exceed the amount of the estimate.

That was the case here and so the appeal was dismissed.

The costs judge should determine how, if at all, to reflect the costs estimate in the assessment *before* going on to decide whether, for reasons unrelated to the estimate, there are elements of the costs claimed which were unreasonably incurred or unreasonable in amount.

This avoids the danger of "double jeopardy" referred to in the context of a discussion about proportionality in *Lownds* v *Home Office* [2002] 1 WLR 2450, [2002] EWCA Civ 365.

While recognising the danger of satellite litigation in relation to the three-part test the court said that *"these concerns do not justify setting at nought the important CPR provisions relating to the making of costs estimates"*.

The court said that a costs *estimate* is not a costs *cap* or a costs *budget* and should not be treated as such, but commented *"there is, however, much to be said for costs budgeting and the capping of costs"*, and referred to the case of *AB* v *Leeds Teaching Hospital NHS Trust (in the matter of the Nationwide Organ Group Litigation)* [2003] EWCH 1034,

High Court, Unreported where a High Court judge made a prospective costs capping order pursuant to the general power conferred by section 51(1) of the Supreme Court Act 1981.

In that case the High Court referred to an earlier decision of the Court of Appeal which it regarded as giving encouragement for the controlling of costs. That case was *Solutia UK Limited* v *Griffiths* [2001] EWCA Civ 736, Court of Appeal where the court said:

> So surely case management powers will allow a judge in the future to exercise the power of limiting costs, either indirectly or even directly, so that they are proportionate to the amount involved. *(Paragraph 29)*

and later, at paragraph 33:

> The present litigation was conducted under the old rules preceding the Woolf reforms. It is to be hoped that subsequent to the Woolf reforms judges conducting cases will make full use of their powers under the Practice Direction about costs, Section 6, which appears in the Civil Procedure White Book 43/PD–006, to obtain estimates of costs and to exercise their powers in respect of cost and case management to keep costs within the bounds of the proportionate in accordance with the overriding objective.

In a crucial passage, likely to influence heavily the development of the law in this area, the Court of Appeal said:

> 34. We recognise that the use of CPR 43 PD para. 6.6 to control costs by taking costs estimates into account at the assessment stage is not the most effective way of controlling the cost of litigation. It seems to us that the prospective fixing of costs budgets is likely to achieve that objective far more effectively. The question of costs budgets was

raised before the Civil Procedure Rule Committee in June 2001. It is contentious and important. The committee decided to explore the issue, but has not reached any conclusion about it. We invite the committee to re-examine the provisions relating to costs estimates to see whether they should be amended to make them more effective in the control of costs; and also to reach a conclusion on the issue of cost budgets.

Costs Capping

No costs-capping case has yet reached the Court of Appeal, although as we have seen that court is clearly well-disposed towards the concept of costs-capping and costs-budgeting.

Several costs capping cases have been dealt with by the High Court.

In *AB* v *Leeds Teaching Hospitals NHS Trust (in the matter of the Nationwide Organ Group Litigation)* [2003] EWHC 1034, Unreported, High Court, 9 May 2003 the Queen's Bench Division of the High Court, sitting as a first instance court, had before it an application by the defendants for an order to cap the costs of the claimants both retrospectively and prospectively, in what was acknowledged by all parties to be a novel procedure.

The case was a multi-party action where a Group Litigation Order had been made and the claims arose out of the retention by various hospitals of organs of deceased children and adults.

The High Court considered in detail the question of whether courts have the power to make such orders and concluded that they did.

Dealing with the recent history of this subject the court said:

7. It is common ground that the Civil Procedure Rules make no reference to a specific power in the court to make a costs cap order. However, it is clear from the Woolf Report that the court, particularly in Multi-Party Actions, is encouraged to take control of costs just as it is to control the management of issues. The Report makes specific reference to a paper by AAS Zuckerman published during the inquiry stage which contained a section entitled "Prospective Budget Setting". Paragraph 12 of that paper reads:

    "One option to be considered is replacing retrospective taxation with prospective budget setting. Under this regime budgets would be set in advance so that the process would have to conform to budgetary constraints, rather than the cost following the process as at present."

8. In Chapter 17, Section IV of the Woolf Report, at paragraphs 32, 56 and 57 there is a further reference to the necessity for the court to take hands-on control of costs at an early stage in Multi-Party Actions. Paragraph 57 contains the following statement:

    "At every stage in the management of the MPS the Judge should consider, with the help of the parties, the potential impact on costs of the directions that are contemplated, and whether these are justified in relation to what is at issue. Parties and their legal representatives, as in other cases on the multi-track, should provide information on costs already incurred and be prepared to estimate the cost of proposed further work."

The court then considered its statutory powers derived from Section 51(1) of the Supreme Court Act 1981 (as amended) and concluded that they were wide.

It also took the view that even before the advent of the Civil Procedure Rules these powers, together with those under Order 62 of the Rules of the Supreme Court, enabled the court to make a pre-emptive order for costs. (See *Joseph Owen Davies v Eli Lilly and Co.* [1987] 1 WLR 1136.)

It also noted that in *R. v The Prime Minister and Others ex parte The Campaign for Nuclear Disarmament* [2002] EWHC 271 the Divisional Court made an order limiting to £25,000.00 the Applicant's liability for costs in the event of costs subsequently being awarded against it. The application in that case was made under CPR Rule 44.3 and the power to make the order sought was not in dispute.

The court then reviewed its powers under the Civil Procedure Rules and noted that Rule 3.1 provided it with exhaustive and wide-ranging general powers of case management to be carried out in accordance with the overriding objective set out in Rule 1.1 and it quoted Rule 1.1(2) which states:

Dealing with cases justly includes so far as is practicable –

(a) Ensuring that the parties are on an equal footing;

(b) Saving expense;

(c) Dealing with the case in ways which are proportionate –

   (i) To the amount of money involved;

   (ii) To the importance of the case;

   (iii) To the complexity of the issues; and

(iv) To the financial position of each party.

The court then noted that Rule 3.1(2)(m) provides it with the power *"to take any other step or make any other order for the purpose of managing the case and furthering the overriding objective,"* and also that the notes to Part 3 of the Civil Procedure Rules at 3.1.8 refer specifically to "Costs Budgeting" and make specific reference to the case of *Solutia UK Limited* v *Griffiths* [2001] EWCA Civ 736.

Civil Procedure Rules 19.10–15 deal with Group Litigation Orders (GLO's) but make no reference to costs whereas Rule 48.6A does deal with costs in Group Litigation Orders but makes no reference to cost capping or cost budgeting.

The court held:

18. Having referred to Section 51 of the 1981 Act, to the various Parts of the CPR which deal with costs, and giving full effect to the overriding objective of the CPR, in my judgment, the court has power to make a costs cap order. In my opinion the general powers of case management and in particular CPR 3.1(2)(m) and 44.3 are sufficiently wide to encompass the making of such an order in both GLOs and other actions. In addition, the provision for Estimates of Costs in the Practice Direction about Costs is, in my view, in keeping with such a power. Further I am fortified by the encouragement provided by the Court of Appeal in *Solutia UK Limited* v *Griffiths* to conclude that in appropriate cases, of which GLOs are prime examples (see those parts of the Woolf Report to which I have previously referred), the court should do so.

19. In my judgment, in cases where GLOs are concerned the desirability of ensuring that costs are kept within bounds makes it unnecessary for

the court to require exceptional circumstances to be shown before exercising its discretion to make a costs cap order. I note that in claims in the administrative field it has been held that there must be exceptional circumstances before a pre-emptive order for costs is made (see *ex parte CND*). However, I see no reason for such a requirement where a costs cap order is sought in a GLO, particularly where there is a risk that costs may become disproportionate and excessive.

The judge proceeded to set a costs cap in relation to each of four component parts:–

1.	Solicitors' costs	£271,250.00
2.	Experts' fees	£50,000.00
3.	Counsels' fees	£170,250.00
4.	Other disbursements	£15,000.00

The decision of Mr. Justice Gage in the above case was followed in *Various Ledward Claimants* v *Kent and Medway Health Authority and East Kent Hospitals NHS Trust* [2003] EWHC 2551 Q.B., Unreported 3 November 2003, Queen's Bench Division of the High Court.

Although this case attracted considerable publicity it added nothing, in legal terms, to the *Nationwide Organs Group Litigation* case.

However it is useful to read as it goes into considerable detail as to charging rates, mark-up, panel membership, firm's overhead calculations, etc. These are of course all conventional costs issues rather than specific to fixed or capped costs but the case is a salutary, and somewhat frightening, reminder that solicitors will be expected to know all about their overheads, profit margins, etc. when making submissions in relation to costs caps and costs budgets.

The cap is of course just that – it is a maximum and not a *fixed* fee. As Mrs. Justice Hallett put it in this case:

> I should emphasise that this is a cap and not a licence to incur costs unnecessarily.

In this case two of the lead claimants were represented under conditional fee agreements and the court did not inquire as to the success fee and nor was it invited to cap the level of success fee.

This follows from the general rule that the percentage success fee does not have to be disclosed until the end of the case, otherwise the opponent would have some idea of the solicitor's assessment of the strength of the case.

I question whether this rule is now of any value. If the courts are to assess in advance, in considerable detail, all aspects of the dispute including the number of witnesses, experts, etc., etc., then surely it is in a position there and then to assess and fix the percentage success fee.

It rather reduces the effectiveness of a costs cap if the defendant knows that the claimant's base costs are capped at, say, £200,000.00, but does not know whether the success fee will be 20% (£40,000.00) or 100% (£200,000.00).

The parties had agreed that there should be no cap in respect of experts' fees but the court indicated that it would consider this of its own motion, saying:

> I should like to add this. The parties, in my view surprisingly, agreed that the court should not fix any cap in respect of experts' fees. If not controlled, experts' fees can very easily escalate. I note that Ms. Loveday in her statement estimates the experts' charges at £172,000.00. This causes me some concern. Permission

of the court to instruct experts in particular disciplines is not a licence to instruct them on a whole range of subjects without thought to the costs involved. I wish to know the amount of fees already expended on experts and the parties' estimates for future fees preferably at the next case management conference, and also shortly before the start of the trial. A copy of those estimates should be sent to the Senior Costs Judge. I further order that any detailed assessment shall be reserved to him. I have borne in mind that my remarks may influence such an assessment.

In *Smart* v *East Cheshire NHS Trust* [2003] EWHC 2806 (QB), Unreported, High Court, 26 November 2003 the same Judge as in the NOGL case, Mr. Justice Gage, dealt with another first instance application by a defendant in a clinical negligence action, but this case involved just a single claimant and thus was not a Group Litigation Order case. The court refused to make an order and held that very different considerations apply in non GLO cases as compared with GLO cases. Liability and causation, but not quantum, had been agreed.

Mr. Justice Gage held, as to jurisdiction,

> Without intending any disrespect to the solicitors who argued the case before me in the NOGL the arguments presented by counsel on this application have been more detailed and in greater depth than those made to me in the NOGL. Nevertheless, having carefully considered the submissions made in this case I see no reason to change my view that the court has jurisdiction to make such orders.

The second issue in this case, but effectively the main one, was as to the test that the court should adopt when deciding whether or not to exercise its powers to make a costs cap order and in particular the scope for such orders outside cases involving group litigation orders (GLOs).

Mr. Justice Gage put the issue like this:

> ... The claimant submits that in cases other than those involving GLOs an order for a costs cap should only be made in exceptional circumstances and where the court is satisfied by evidence that there is a substantial risk that without such an order costs will be disproportionately and/or unreasonably incurred or be disproportionate and/or unreasonable in amount; and conventional case management and detailed assessment of costs may not be effective in managing and limiting the extent of costs.
>
> The defendant submits that the court may make an order in an appropriate case; that is any case where there is a significant danger that costs may become excessive or disproportionate and it is just to make such an order.

The claimant pointed out the absence of any reference to costs cap orders in *Lownds* v *Home Office* [2002] 1 WLR 2450, [2002] EWCA Civ 365, Court of Appeal and sought to distinguish the *NOGL* and *Ledward Claimants* cases on the basis that both of those cases involved GLOs and not "conventional ordinary litigation".

The claimant further relied upon three decisions of the Administrative Court all holding that a pre-emptive costs order should only be made in exceptional circumstances. Those cases are:

- *R.* v *Lord Chancellor ex parte CPAG* [1998] 2 AER 755, High Court Administrative Court

- *R.* v *London Borough of Hammersmith and Fulham ex parte CPRE* [2000] ENVLR 544, High Court Administrative Court

- *R.* v *Prime Minister and Others ex parte CND* [2002] EWHC 2712, High Court Administrative Court.

The claimant argued that a costs cap order is a form of pre-emptive costs order and was thus covered by these cases.

The defendant relied on the *NOGL* and *Ledward Claimants* decisions saying that once the power to make a costs cap order is assumed it is illogical to write in a requirement of exceptional circumstances before an order can be made in ordinary litigation.

It sought to distinguish the Administrative Court decisions on the basis that they deal with a public interest situation and have no relevance to cases such as this one.

The court took the view that the three Administrative Court decisions support the proposition that the court has jurisdiction to make pre-emptive orders for costs in non-GLO cases but only in exceptional circumstances, but that, whilst of assistance, these cases were not determinative of the way that the court's discretion should be exercised when dealing with costs cap applications.

The court set out the following guidelines for non-GLO cases:

> The court should only consider making a costs cap order in such cases where the applicant shows by evidence that there is a real and substantial risk that without such an order costs will be disproportionately or unreasonably incurred; and that this risk may not be managed by conventional case management and a detailed assessment of costs after a trial; and it is just to make such an order. It seems to me that it is unnecessary to ascribe to such a test the general heading of exceptional circumstances. I would expect that in the run of ordinary actions it will be rare for this test to be satisfied but it is impossible to predict all the circumstances in which it may be said to arise. Low value claims will inevitably mean a higher proportion of costs to value than high value claims. Some high value claims will involve greater factual and legal

complexities than others. Clinical negligence cases, for example, will involve more complicated issues on liability than personal injury cases arising out of road traffic accidents. In my judgment, it would be quite wrong to attempt to set a specified ratio of costs to value for any particular type or class of case. I stress, in my opinion, each case must be considered on its own facts. In those circumstances, it seems to me very unlikely that it would be appropriate for the court to adopt a practice of capping costs in the majority of clinical negligence cases.

The judge made it clear that these considerations did not apply to group litigation in which cases *"the court has a clear duty ...... to manage the litigation from an early stage in such a way that one or other party does not allow costs to spiral out of control"*.

In declining to make a costs cap order in this case the judge gave guidance as to how such applications, in non-GLO cases, should be dealt with in the future.

First, when an application is made it must be supported by evidence showing a prima facie case that the test can be satisfied. It will generally not be sufficient to assert that in the type of case being dealt with costs can spiral out of control.

Secondly, the allocation and listing questionnaires if properly and carefully completed by the parties will have attached estimates of costs incurred to date and the likely overall costs. In substantial cases these must be provided in accordance with the Practice Direction to Part 43 (CPS Section 6 Estimates of Costs, in particular 6.1 and 6.6). These should give a good guide to the costs of each party.

Thirdly, if such an application comes before the court it should be possible to deal with it at a comparatively short hearing. Nothing could be worse than a proliferation of applications occupying much court time and giving rise

to costly satellite litigation. (See for example *Giambrone* v
JMC Holidays [2002] EWHC 2932.)

Fourthly, the benefit of the doubt in respect of the
reasonableness of prospective costs should be resolved in
favour of the party being capped.

The order should include a provision for uplift in certain
specified circumstances. In that way it ought to be
possible to limit the issues on a detailed assessment and
in many cases to avoid a hearing altogether.

In this way, a costs cap order may become a useful tool in
the court's armoury for preventing, in an appropriate
case, costs spiralling out of control and reducing the costs
of post-trial assessments.

CHAPTER 8
COURT OF PROTECTION

CHAPTER 8
COURT OF PROTECTION

On 9 December 2003 a Practice Note was issued by D.A. Lush, Master of the Court of Protection, in the following terms:

Court of Protection Practice Note: Solicitors fixed costs

It has been agreed with the Law Society that fixed costs will be allowed at amounts not exceeding the following:

Category I

Work up to and including the date upon which the First General Order or Short Order is entered – £665 (plus VAT). (The commencement fee, appointment fee, and fees for medical evidence and evidence of notification of the patient may be added. Please produce receipts for fees paid.)

Category II

(a) Preparation and lodgment of a receivership account – £175 (plus VAT)

(b) Preparation and lodgment of a receivership account which has been certified by a solicitor under the provisions of the Practice Notes dated 13 September 1984 and 5 March 1985 reported at [1984] 3 All ER 320 and [1985] 1 All ER 884 respectively – £190 (plus VAT).

Category III

General management work in the second and subsequent years

(a) where there are lay receivers and the Court has authorised the receiver to employ solicitors to carry out work not usually requiring professional assistance under rule 87 of the Court of Protection Rules 2001 – £520 (plus VAT)

(b) where there are professional receivers – £590 (plus VAT).

(Note: Categories II and III may be claimed together.)

Category IV

Applications under sections 36(9) or 54 of the Trustee Act 1925 for the appointment of a new trustee in the place of the patient – £320 (plus VAT).

Category V

In respect of conveyancing two elements will be allowable as follows:

(a) A sum of £125 in every case to cover correspondence with the Public Guardianship Office, the preparation of the certificate or affidavit of value and all other work solely attributable to the Court of Protection or the Public Guardianship Office, together with

(b) a value element of $\frac{1}{2}$% of the consideration up to £400,000 and $\frac{1}{4}$% thereafter, with a minimum sum for this element of £330.

As well as a fee for both the above elements, VAT and disbursements will be allowed.

New rates of fixed costs will apply as follows:–

in Category I, to all draft First General Orders sent out on or after 1 January 2004

in Category II, to all receivership accounts lodged on or after 1 January 2004

in Category III, to all general management costs in respect of years ended on or after 1 January 2004

in Category IV, to all orders sent out on or after 1 January 2004

The amounts stated for each category are the maximum sum that may be claimed. If the value of the work is less than the maximum sum allowed, professionals may accept the lower amount without further reference to the Court.

In all categories, professionals will have the option of the Costs Officer carrying out a detailed assessment of the costs under Category II as well as Category III, the relevant items for both categories should be included in the same bill.

D.A. Lush, Master of the Court of Protection

9 December 2003

Comment

The statement is rather confused, possibly because few of those involved in the legal system are prepared to take the psychological step of abandoning the hourly rate altogether.

Thus although the Practice Note is entitled "Solicitors fixed costs" it will be seen that in fact solicitors retain the option of the Costs Officer carrying out a detailed assessment of the costs rather than accepting fixed costs (see final paragraph of note).

Furthermore the costs are in fact *capped* and not *fixed*.

The opening sentence says:

> "It has been agreed with the Law Society that fixed costs will be allowed at amounts *not exceeding* (my emphasis) the following:"

In case there was any doubt about its interpretation the penultimate paragraph states:–

> "The amounts stated for each category are the maximum that may be claimed. If the value of the work is less than the maximum sum allowed, professionals may accept the lower amount without further reference to the Court."

Thus if actual costs are *lower* than the costs set out in the Practice Note then that *lower* sum is payable, albeit without reference to the Court.

This produces the bizarre scenario that provided the solicitor comes in at, say, £1 less than the "fixed" costs then he or she receives that sum "without further reference to the Court".

One wonders what this Practice Note achieves. If the costs are in excess of the "fixed" costs then the solicitor can claim the higher sum through detailed assessment if they are lower then the solicitor only gets that lower sum.

It is not clear what happens if the solicitor wishes to claim fixed costs. As we have seen a figure *below* "fixed" costs can be accepted "without further reference to the Court" and a figure *above* "fixed" costs is to be the subject of detailed assessment.

What about actual "fixed" costs?

As an example of muddled thinking this Practice Note takes some beating.

In future it would be helpful if the Law Society and the courts consulted people who actually understood the principles of fixed costs.

CHAPTER 9
THE FUTURE

CHAPTER 9
THE FUTURE

Fixed costs are likely to spread rapidly to other areas of law, such as workplace accidents and public liability cases, and the restriction of their use to unissued, low-value claims in any given field is likely to disappear. Success fees in road traffic accidents are now to be fixed, whatever the value of the claim and whether the claim settles or goes to trial.

This increase in the use of fixed costs will be achieved partly through direct changes to the Civil Procedure Rules and Practice Directions and partly through judicial interpretation of existing rules (see Chapter 7, *Costs Controls by the Courts*) and partly through agreement between claimant and defendant lawyers and insurers.

The next jurisdiction to be covered by fixed costs is almost certain to be workplace accidents up to £15,000.00 in value.

In its final report on its review of employers' liability compulsory insurance the Department for Work and Pensions suggested that the fixed fee scheme currently operating for road traffic accident cases be extended to workplace accidents.

The Department has for some time been concerned that the cost of employers' liability insurance is driving firms out of business, or causing them to "offshore" to avoid the extent and cost of litigation in the United Kingdom. At Page 12 of its final report it says:

> Legal costs and the process of resolving claims can be most disproportionate in relation to smaller claims. Therefore action is aimed primarily at smaller, low complexity claims. ...... The challenge is to remove frictional costs ...... by reducing the number of interactions between parties needed to resolve a particular claim.

The Times, 9 December 2003, carried this news report:

> Plans to bring in fixed fees for workplace accident claims are being resisted by the Association of Personal Injury Lawyers. With government reforms pending on employers' liability insurance, the association says that it is too soon to consider the plans. It backs the fixed-fee scheme for low-value traffic claims but says that workplace claims are a "much more complex area of the law".

The report anticipates a pilot scheme for fixed fees in employers' liability cases being introduced in June 2004. That is unlikely in my view but they are likely to be in place by Spring 2005. However as with road traffic accident cases fixed percentage success fees may well be in place by the end of 2004.

The Department commissioned research on costs and success fees in Employers' Liability (EL) and Public Liability (PL) claims and this research was published by the Department for Constitutional Affairs (DCA) on 4 December 2003 under the title *Costs of Low Value EL Claims 1997–2002* by Paul Fenn and Neil Rickman.

The findings include that:

- base costs of EL cases rise proportionately with damages in a fairly predictable manner up to a case value of approximately £10,000.00.

- between 2000–2002 EL accident claims appear to have been fairly constant in volume terms and combined claimant costs and disbursements for sub-£15,000 accident claims increased from approximately £2,000.00 to approximately £2,800.00 between 2000 and 2002, during a period when average damages were constant at £3,000.00.

- the increase in total costs including disbursements was much larger in non-litigated EL cases than litigated ones between 2000 and 2002, perhaps indicating a "Woolf-effect" due to front-loading. This appears consistent with the effect of Woolf on the "front-loading" of case-work (which needs to be balanced against the fact that more claims are settling without the need for issue of court proceedings).

- there is little difference between Conditional Fee Agreement and non CFA EL claims with respect to the level and growth rates of mean agreed total costs including disbursements, success fees and After-the-Event Insurance premia. Thus the costs increases cannot be readily ascribed to the recoverability of success fees and insurance premia introduced on 1 April 2000.

Given the widespread, and in my opinion accurate, view that the Woolf Reforms have increased costs the Department for Work and Pensions has set out some ideas for reducing work and therefore costs and these include:

- Reducing delay and duplication throughout the process: cutting down delay between the incident itself and insurer notification and investigation. Currently there can be delays between the date an accident occurs and the date that a letter of intention to claim is sent to an employer and subsequently an insurer. This can mean that evidence gathering and decisions as to liability become unnecessarily protracted.

- Reducing duplication of investigation into the circumstances of the accident first by the claimant solicitor and then by the insurer once they are notified of the claim.

- Streamlining the process of gathering data from the other party as part of this investigation which can often be lengthy and unnecessarily adversarial.

- Improving staff experience to reduce the likelihood of log-jams in the system. Many claims seem to get to a certain point where unnecessary friction has built up on both sides and there is lengthy sequential correspondence dealing with, for example, questions of contributory negligence on comparatively small sums. This leads to delays and confrontation which prevent settlement and often add unnecessary cost.

The report mentions a number of options to tackle these issues in relation to smaller claims:

- **Incident** – standardisation of the initial accident report to meet the needs of recipients (HSE and insurers) should cut out duplication of recording.

- **Notification** – Employers, once notified of an incident that may or may not give rise to a claim, could immediately notify their insurers who would then be able to investigate the circumstances of an accident and the question of liability.

- **Investigation** – standardisation of a form to record full circumstances of the incident and the nature, extent and severity of injuries to save subsequent investigation.

- **Communication and information exchange** – Greater use of the telephone in particular as well as electronic methods of communication such as e-mail by parties in the resolution process, with correspondence used purely for formal confirmation, to speed up the process.

- **Staff Expertise** – Having a senior point of upward referral for both insurers and solicitors would enable someone with a fresh pair of eyes to look at the case objectively. Such a person would have the authority to negotiate and settle these claims quickly once the claim had remained outstanding for a set period of time.

- **Legal Advice** – One suggestion option could be for any proposed settlement in lower value claims to include provision for employees to seek legal advice to check that the settlement is fair, but otherwise for the insurer or employer to deal directly with the claimant. Where the claim is more complex, then a greater degree of legal input is likely to be necessary. Employees would retain the right to litigate should they so choose, for instance if they were not satisfied with a decision on liability or on settlement levels.

The report states:

> The Government will now work with stakeholders to develop ways of putting these proposals into practice. In most cases, we believe that the best way to start to do this will be to develop pilot schemes which will enable us to test and evaluate the practicality and outcomes of new approaches. If successful, such approaches could then be applied more generally, perhaps by establishing Codes of Practice between insurers and clients or between insurers and lawyers, in particular to cover the crucial early stages of any claim, before the pre-action protocol comes into effect.

The first and fastest way to make progress might be to seek to work with a large, heavily unionised employer, with a single insurer and a key interest claims solicitor. But we will also look closely at ways to extend our piloting to smaller businesses – either collectively or singly. Our intention in all cases is to use pilots, whether with large or small businesses, to develop approaches which can be applied generally. For this reason we will be closely involving the Federation of Small Businesses and a major insurer specialising in underwriting SMEs in the development of our proposals.

Compromise Agreements

Significantly the Department for Work and Pensions goes much further than simply suggesting fixed costs in workplace accidents but challenges the whole concept of lawyers being involved throughout such cases, proposing instead something akin to the compromise agreement system used in employment tribunal cases.

It says that claimant personal injury solicitors should only have a role in checking settlements of lower-value workplace accident cases and then work under fixed fees in other cases. The Department's primary concern is to save costs for employers.

One option put forward by the Department is that any proposed settlement in lower-value claims shall include provision for employees to seek legal advice to check that it is fair, but otherwise for the insurer or employer to deal directly with the claimant, adding that "where the claim is more complex, then a greater deal of legal input is likely to be necessary".

In Employment Tribunal cases parties are free not to be legally represented and indeed most are not represented. However they are not free to agree a binding settlement without the applicant receiving advice from a qualified lawyer.

If the parties agree such settlement without the applicant receiving such advice then it is not binding upon the applicant who thus can take the settlement money and still issue or continue with employment tribunal proceedings.

Because of this a custom has developed whereby employers wishing to compromise claims agree to pay for the employee to receive such advice in relation to the compromise agreement.

The sums paid vary enormously from around £250.00 to several thousand pounds in more complex cases.

Section 203 of the Employment Rights Act 1996, which governs compromise agreements in employment matters, appears as Appendix C of this book.

The introduction of compromise agreements into personal injury work is likely to lead to a significant increase in work for high-street firms and a reduction in work for bulk providers, especially firms doing only, or mainly, trade union work.

If the requirement of a compromise agreement was introduced into *all* personal injury work then there would be considerable benefits to the public and to lawyers.

The vast majority of settlements is reached without the intervention of lawyers and this is especially so in road traffic accidents. If *all* settlements had to receive the sanction of a compromise agreement, paid for by the liability insurers, then there would never be any under-settlement of cases by clients representing themselves. If the solicitor wrongly advised the lay client in relation to a settlement then the client would have a remedy against the solicitor. Thus the introduction of compromise agreements would represent a huge advance in consumer protection. Indeed it would be the most vulnerable, that is those not in trades unions and not aware of legal expenses insurance etc., who would benefit most.

The new Motor Insurers' Bureau Scheme in relation to compensation of victims of untraced drivers provides a model for such a scheme (see Chapter 7: The Motor Insurers' Bureau Contingency Fee Scheme).

Under that scheme the Motor Insurers' Bureau pays a fee to the claimant/applicant's solicitor of £500.00 plus VAT or 15% of the award, whichever is greater, and with a cap of £3,000.00 on awards of between £20,000.00 and £150,000.00. VAT is added to the costs figures.

This could provide the basis for compromise agreements in road traffic accident cases and indeed one could use exactly the same tariff, but with no cap, so that the fixed fee would be the greater of £500.00 plus VAT or 15% of the damages, payable by the liability insurer.

Clearly the higher the damages the less likely it is that a client will be representing him or herself but if the client chooses to do so then this scheme provides a significant safety net.

Example

Dennis Damaged is dealing with his claim himself and the insurers have offered £10,000.00. The solicitor's fee will be £1,500.00 (15% of £10,000.00). Thus the solicitor has considerable scope to investigate the claim – about nine hours' work at today's rates for a Grade 1 solicitor.

By comparison the fee under the fixed costs scheme for such a case would be £2,550.00, but of course much more work will have been done for that higher fee.

At the lower end of the scale the minimum fee of £500.00 provides for around three hours' work on even the simplest of cases and settlements. Often an experienced solicitor will be able to deal with the case in a fraction of that time.

The minimum fee under the fixed costs scheme is £1,000.00 but to earn that fee the solicitor will have done far more work.

Furthermore the fixed costs scheme only kicks in once the claim is cost-bearing, that is when damages are over £1,000.00 in personal injury cases and over £5,000.00 in damage-only cases.

The compromise agreement scheme should apply to *all* cases, whatever their value, as it does in employment tribunals, and thus far more cases would be covered. Arguably it is the lay client accepting a very low sum who is in most need of qualified legal advice to ensure that he or she is not undersettling.

These costs would be payable by the liability insurers.

The MIB scheme is based on the assumption that the solicitor will do relatively little work as the MIB is obliged to undertake most of the work:

Clause 7(1)   *"MIB shall, at its own cost, take all reasonable steps to investigate the claim ......".*

In a compromise agreement it will be the lay client who has done most of the work but the principle is the same – the solicitor is paid for checking the agreement and the client has the security of that advice and of the solicitor's professional indemnity insurance.

In more complex cases, such as workplace accidents, the minimum figure could be increased to allow a greater amount of time to be justified in checking the settlement, say £750.00 or 20% of the award, whichever is greater.

Clients would still be free to instruct solicitors to conduct the whole case but with a fixed costs regime in place.

One option is to increase the small claims track limit to £5,000.00 in all cases, in other words to bring personal injury in line with other types of action, and to allow only a compromise agreement fee for small claims track work.

There will always be a compromise agreement, even if the solicitor has dealt with the case from the beginning, as that is the way the case is settled. The only exception is if the matter goes to trial, but provision could be made for a fixed trial fee equivalent to the compromise agreement fee.

There are powerful arguments in favour of compromise agreements in all personal injury cases, primarily because a lay client is almost always up against a rich and powerful insurance company.

Lawyers who are seriously concerned about the public should look more closely at compromise agreements and not just at their own bank balances.

Conditional Fees and Compromise Agreements

As the solicitor is not at risk of carrying out considerable work for no fee there is no reason why compromise agreement fees should attract a success fee and nor is after-the-event insurance necessary.

Conditional Fees

As costs become fixed in progressively more cases then conditional fees are likely to disappear as the extra element related to risk will be incorporated into the standard fee.

After all is there now a single solicitor in the country doing claimant personal injury work and getting paid in full in the event of defeat?[1]

All claimant personal injury work is now done on a conditional fee basis, whether it be trade union work, legal expenses insurance or whatever. The difference is between those who get a success fee and those who take the risk for no extra fee in return for a regular supply of work from an insurer, trade union, etc.

This is happening in road traffic accidents, where "fixed" success fees will be introduced this year (2004) *and not just in relation to fixed costs cases.*

In all road traffic cases worth £500,000.00 or less the solicitor's success fee will be fixed at 12.5% for cases that settle and 100% for those that reach trial.

Barristers will be subject to the same arrangement save that an extra tier has been added for cases that settle shortly before trial. Thus barristers, but only barristers, will receive a 75% success fee when a road traffic case settles within 21 days of a multi-track trial and a 50% success fee when a road traffic case settles within 14 days of a fast-track trial.

Even for cases involving more than £500,000.00 the starting point is that there will be a 12.5% success fee as above but there will be an "escape clause" in such cases allowing for a potentially higher success fee on settlement.

In practice cases of such high value are few and far between and therefore from a practice management point of view it can be assumed that the success fee will now be fixed in all road traffic cases.

Rules brought these proposals into effect with effect from 1 March 2004 in relation to cases covered by fixed

---

1. OK, yes there is. The occasional client with legal expenses insurance who instructs a non-panel solicitor who manages to persuade the legal expenses insurer to fund the case win or lose. It does not happen very often!

recoverable costs (that is unissued road traffic accident claims worth £10,000.00 or less and where the cause of action arose on or after 6 October 2003) and with effect from 1 June 2004 or shortly thereafter in all other road traffic cases.

These rules are not retrospective and for a consideration of the success fee in fixed costs cases taken on before 1 March 2004 please see Chapter 4, *Fixed Costs and Conditional Fees*.

This is another significant step – the fixing of part of the costs – the success fee – in relation to all road traffic cases, *whatever their value*.

It should be noted that in cases covered by the existing fixed-costs scheme, that is unissued road traffic accident claims of £10,000.00 or less, counsel's base fee is *not* treated as a disbursement and comes out of the solicitor's fixed costs, that is it operates as a deduction from the solicitor's fee. Counsel's success fee is free-standing and will *not* be deducted from the solicitor's costs, except in the sense that had the solicitor carried out the work he or she would have earnt the success fee as well as the base fee.

In non-fixed costs cases counsel's fee is a disbursement.

Non-Personal Injury Work

The first area of work that is outside the road traffic or personal injury field that is likely to be covered by fixed costs is housing disrepair cases.

The housing disrepair market has many similarities to the road traffic accident market – work is often supplied by referrers, it is done in bulk and the defendants are "repeat players" as with liability insurers in road traffic accident cases. The "repeat players" in housing disrepair cases tend to be local authorities.

There is scope for agreement between individual firms of claimant solicitors and local authorities. The work is predictable and a "swings and roundabouts" approach to costs would introduce certainty for everyone and allow claimants' solicitors to streamline their processes and become more efficient without sacrificing profit, thus achieving lower costs to the public sector in housing but maintaining or improving solicitors' profitability.

Standing Canute-like[2] against the tide of fixed costs will achieve nothing and lawyers need to plan now for a fixed fee future.

---

2. King Canute has had a very bad press. He was in fact demonstrating to his followers that he had no power over the sea, *not* vainly trying to show that he did have such power.

APPENDICES

APPENDIX A
PART 45 OF THE C.P.R.

Fixed Costs

APPENDIX A
PART 45 OF THE C.P.R.

Fixed Costs

Scope of this Section

45.1 (1) This Section sets out the amounts which, unless the court orders otherwise, are to be allowed in respect of solicitors' charges in the cases to which this Section applies.

(2) This Section applies where –

(a) the only claim is a claim for a specified sum of money where the value of the claim exceeds £25 and –

(i) judgment in default is obtained under rule 12.4(1);

(ii) judgment on admission is obtained under rule 14.4(3);

(iii) judgment on admission on part of the claim is obtained under rule 14.5(6);

(iv) summary judgment is given under Part 24;

(v) the court has made an order to strike out (GL) a defence under rule 3.4(2)(a) as disclosing no reasonable grounds for defending the claim; or

(vi) rule 45.3 applies; or

(b) the only claim is a claim where the court gave a fixed date for the hearing when it issued the claim and judgment is given for the delivery of goods, and the value of the claim exceeds £25; or

(c) a judgment creditor has taken steps under Parts 70 to 73 to enforce a judgment or order.

(The practice direction supplementing rule 7.9 sets out the types of case where a court may give a fixed date for a hearing when it issues a claim)

(3) Any appropriate court fee will be allowed in addition to the costs set out in this Part.

Amount of fixed commencement costs

45.2   (1) The claim form may include a claim for fixed commencement costs.

(2) The amount of fixed commencement costs which the claim form may include shall be calculated by reference to the following table (Table 1).

(3) Additional costs may also be claimed in the circumstances specified in Table 3.

(4) The amount claimed, or the value of the goods claimed if specified, in the claim form is to be used for determining the band in the table that applies to the claim.

Table 1

Fixed costs on commencement of a claim			
Relevant band	Where the claim form is served by the court or by any method other than personal service by the claimant	Where • the claim form is served personally by the claimant; and • there is only one defendant	Where there is more than one defendant, for each additional defendant personally served at separate addresses by the claimant
Where – • the value of the claim exceeds £25 but does not exceed £500	£50	£60	£15
Where – • the value of the claim exceeds £500 but does not exceed £1,000	£70	£80	£15

Fixed costs on commencement of a claim			
Relevant band	Where the claim form is served by the court or by any method other than personal service by the claimant	Where • the claim form is served personally by the claimant; and • there is only one defendant	Where there is more than one defendant, for each additional defendant personally served at separate addresses by the claimant
Where – • the value of the claim exceeds £1,000 but does not exceed £5,000; or • the only claim is for delivery of goods and no value is specified or stated on the claim form	£80	£90	£15
Where – • the value of the claim exceeds £5,000	£100	£110	£15

When defendant only liable for fixed commencement costs

45.3   (1) Where –

(a) the only claim is for a specified sum of money; and

(b) the defendant pays the money claimed within 14 days after service of particulars of claim on him, together with the fixed commencement costs stated in the claim form,

the defendant is not liable for any further costs unless the court orders otherwise.

(2) Where –

(a) the claimant gives notice of acceptance of a payment into court in satisfaction of the whole claim;

(b) the only claim is for a specified sum of money; and

(c) the defendant made the payment into court within 14 days after service of the particulars of claim on him, together with the fixed costs stated in the claim form,

the defendant is not liable for any further costs unless the court orders otherwise.

Costs on entry of judgment

45.4   Where –

(a) the claimant has claimed fixed commencement costs under rule 45.2; and

(b) judgment is entered in the circumstances specified in the table in this rule (Table 2), the amount to be included in the judgment in respect of the claimant's solicitor's charges is the aggregate of –

(i) the fixed commencement costs; and

(ii) the relevant amount shown in Table 2.

Table 2

Fixed costs on Entry of Judgment		
	Where the amount of the judgment exceeds £25 but does not exceed £5,000	Where the amount of the judgment exceeds £5,000
Where judgment in default of an acknowledgment of service is entered under rule 12.4(1) (entry of judgment by request on claim for money only)	£22	£30
Where judgment in default of a defence is entered under rule 12.4(1) (entry of judgment by request on claim for money only)	£25	£35

Fixed costs on Entry of Judgment		
	Where the amount of the judgment exceeds £25 but does not exceed £5,000	Where the amount of the judgment exceeds £5,000
Where judgment is entered under rule 14.4 (judgment on admission), or rule 14.5 (judgment on admission of part of claim) and claimant accepts the defendant's proposal as to the manner of payment	£40	£55
Where judgment is entered under rule 14.4 (judgment on admission), or rule 14.5 (judgment on admission on part of claim) and court decides the date or times of payment	£55	£70
Where summary judgment is given under Part 24 or the court strikes out a defence under rule 3.4(2)(a), in either case, on application by a party	£175	£210
Where judgment is given on a claim for delivery of goods under a regulated agreement within the meaning of the Consumer Credit Act 1974 and no other entry in this table applies	£60	£85

Miscellaneous fixed costs

45.5   The table in this rule (Table 3) shows the amount to be allowed in respect of solicitor's charges in the circumstances mentioned.

Table 3

Miscellaneous Fixed Costs	
For service by a party of any document required to be served personally including preparing and copying a certificate of service for each individual served	£15
Where service by an alternative method is permitted by an order under rule 6.8 for each individual served	£25
Where a document is served out of the jurisdiction – (a) in Scotland, Northern Ireland, the Isle of Man or the Channel Islands; (b) in any other place	£65 £75

Fixed enforcement costs

45.6   The table in this rule (Table 4) shows the amount to be allowed in respect of solicitors' costs in the circumstances mentioned. The amounts shown in Table 3 are to be allowed in addition, if applicable.

Table 4

Fixed Enforcement Costs	
For an application under rule 70.5(4) that an award may be enforced as if payable under a court order, where the amount outstanding under the award:	
exceeds £25 but does not exceed £250	£30.75
exceeds £250 but does not exceed £600	£41.00
exceeds £600 but does not exceed £2,000	£69.50
exceeds £2,000	£75.50
On attendance to question a judgment debtor (or officer of a company or other corporation) who has been ordered to attend court under rule 71.2 where the questioning takes place before a court officer, including attendance by a responsible representative of the solicitor.	for each half-hour or part, £15.00 (When the questioning takes place before a judge, he may summarily assess any costs allowed.)
On the making of a final third party debt order under rule 72.8(6)(a) or an order for the payment to the judgment creditor of money in court under rule 72.10(1)(b): if the amount recovered is less than £150 otherwise £98.50 one-half of the amount recovered On the making of a final charging order under rule 73.8(2)(a): £110.00	The court may also allow reasonable disbursements in respect of search fees and the registration of the order.

APPENDIX B
PART 45 OF THE C.P.R.

Road Traffic Accidents – Fixed Recoverable Costs in Costs-Only Proceedings

APPENDIX B
PART 45 OF THE C.P.R.

Road Traffic Accidents – Fixed Recoverable Costs in Costs-Only Proceedings

Scope and interpretation

45.7   (1) This Section sets out the costs which are to be allowed in costs-only proceedings in cases to which this Section applies.

(Costs-only proceedings are issued using the procedure set out in rule 44.12A)

(2) This Section applies where –

(a) the dispute arises from a road traffic accident;

(b) the agreed damages include damages in respect of personal injury, damage to property, or both;

(c) the total value of the agreed damages does not exceed £10,000; and

(d) if a claim had been issued for the amount of the agreed damages, the small claims track would not have been the normal track for that claim.

(3) This Section does not apply where the claimant is a litigant in person.

(Rule 2.3 defines 'personal injuries' as including any disease and any impairment of a person's physical or mental condition)

(Rule 26.6 provides for when the small claims track is the normal track)

(4) In this Section –

(a) 'road traffic accident' means an accident resulting in bodily injury to any person or damage to property caused by, or arising out of, the use of a motor vehicle on a road or other public place in England and Wales;

(b) 'motor vehicle' means a mechanically propelled vehicle intended for use on roads; and

(c) 'road' means any highway and any other road to which the public has access and includes bridges over which a road passes.

Application of fixed recoverable costs

45.8   Subject to rule 45.12, the only costs which are to be allowed are –

(a) fixed recoverable costs calculated in accordance with rule 45.9;

(b) disbursements allowed in accordance with rule 45.10; and

      (c) a success fee allowed in accordance with rule 45.11.

      (Rule 45.12 provides for where a party issues a claim for more than the fixed recoverable costs)

Amount of fixed recoverable costs

45.9   (1) Subject to paragraphs (2) and (3), the amount of fixed recoverable costs is the total of –

      (a) £800;

      (b) 20% of the damages agreed up to £5,000; and

      (c) 15% of the damages agreed between £5,000 and £10,000.

    (2) Where the claimant –

      (a) lives or works in an area set out in the relevant practice direction; and

      (b) instructs a solicitor or firm of solicitors who practise in that area,

    the fixed recoverable costs shall include, in addition to the costs specified in paragraph (1), an amount equal to 12.5% of the costs allowable under that paragraph.

    (3) Where appropriate, value added tax (VAT) may be recovered in addition to the amount of fixed recoverable costs and any reference in this Section to fixed recoverable costs is a reference to those costs net of any such VAT.

Disbursements

45.10 (1) The court –

(a) may allow a claim for a disbursement of a type mentioned in paragraph (2); but

(b) must not allow a claim for any other type of disbursement.

(2) The disbursements referred to in paragraph (1) are –

(a) the cost of obtaining –

(i)   medical records;

(ii) a medical report;

(iii) a police report;

(iv) an engineer's report; or

(v) a search of the records of the Driver Vehicle Licensing Authority;

(b) the amount of an insurance premium; or, where a body of a prescribed description within the meaning of section 30(1) of the Access to Justice Act 1999 undertakes to meet liabilities incurred to pay the costs of other parties to proceedings, a sum not exceeding such additional amount of costs as would be allowed under section 30 in respect of provision made against the risk of having to meet such liabilities[1];

---

1. *The Civil Procedure (Amendment) (No 5) Rules 2003 provide the following Explanatory Note:* Rule 45.10 is amended to clarify that, in costs-only proceedings brought under Section II of Part 45 by a party funded by a body which indemnifies its members or other persons against liabilities for costs which they may incur in proceedings, the court may allow that party as a disbursement a sum not exceeding such amount as would be allowed under section 30 of the Access to Justice Act 1999.

(c) where they are necessarily incurred by reason of one or more of the claimants being a child or patient as defined in Part 21 –

(i) fees payable for instructing counsel; or

(ii) court fees payable on an application to the court;

(d) any other disbursement that has arisen due to a particular feature of the dispute.

('insurance premium' is defined in rule 43.2)

Success fee

45.11   (1) A claimant may recover a success fee if he has entered into a funding arrangement of a type specified in rule 43.2(k)(i).

(2) The amount of the success fee shall be 12.5% of the fixed recoverable costs calculated in accordance with rule 45.9(1), disregarding any additional amount which may be included in the fixed recoverable costs by virtue of rule 45.9(2).[2]

(Rule 43.2(k)(i) defines as funding arrangement as including a conditional fee agreement or collective conditional fee agreement which provides for a success fee)

---

2.   *The Civil Procedure (Amendment) (No 5) Rules 2003 provide the following Explanatory Note:* Rule 45.11 is amended to specify the amount of the success fee which a claimant may recover in proceedings under Section II of Part 45 if he has entered into a conditional fee agreement or a collective conditional fee agreement which provides for a success fee.

Claims for an amount of costs exceeding fixed recoverable costs

45.12 (1) The court will entertain a claim for an amount of costs (excluding any success fee or disbursements) greater than the fixed recoverable costs but only if it considers that there are exceptional circumstances making it appropriate to do so.

(2) If the court considers such a claim appropriate, it may –

(a) assess the costs; or

(b) make an order for the costs to be assessed.

(3) If the court does not consider the claim appropriate, it must make an order for fixed recoverable costs only.

Failure to achieve costs greater than fixed recoverable costs

45.13 (1) This rule applies where –

(a) costs are assessed in accordance with rule 45.12(2); and

(b) the court assesses the costs (excluding any VAT) as being an amount which is less than 20% greater than the amount of the fixed recoverable costs.

(2) The court must order the defendant to pay to the claimant the lesser of –

(a) the fixed recoverable costs; and

(b) the assessed costs.

Costs of the costs-only proceedings

45.14   Where –

(a) the court makes an order for fixed recoverable costs in accordance with rule 45.12(3); or

(b) rule 45.13 applies,

the court must –

(i)   make no award for the payment of the claimant's costs in bringing the proceedings under rule 44.12A; and

(ii) order that the claimant pay the defendant's costs of defending those proceedings.

Directions Relating to Part 45

Section 25A – Road Traffic Accidents: Fixed Recoverable Costs in Costs-only Proceedings

Scope

25A.1   Section II of Part 45 ('the Section') provides for certain fixed costs to be recoverable between parties in respect of costs incurred in disputes which are settled prior to proceedings being issued. The Section applies to road traffic accident disputes as defined in rule 45.7(4)(a), where the accident which gave rise to the dispute occurred on or after 6th October 2003.

25A.2   The Section does not apply to diputes where the total agreed value of the damages is within the small claims limit or exceeds £10,000. Rule 26.8(2) sets out how the financial value of a claim is assessed for the purposes of allocation to track.

25A.3   Fixed recoverable costs are to be calculated by reference to the amount of agreed damages which are payable to the receiving party. In calculating the amount of these damages –

(a) account must be taken of both general and special damages and interest;

(b) any interim payments made must be included;

(c) where the parties have agreed an element of contributory negligence, the amount of damages attributed to that negligence must be deducted;

(d) any amount required by statute to be paid by the compensating party directly to a third party (such as sums paid by way of compensation recovery payments and National Health Service expenses) must not be included.

25A.4   The Section applies to cases which fall within the scope of the Uninsured Drivers Agreement dated 13 August 1999. The section does not apply to cases which fall within the scope of the Untraced Drivers Agreement dated 14 February 2003.

Fixed recoverable costs formula

25A.5   The amount of fixed costs recoverable is calculated by totalling the following –

(a) the sum of £800;

(b) 20% of the agreed damages up to £5,000; and

(c) 15% of the agreed damages between £5,000 and £10,000.

For example, agreed damages of £7,523 would result in recoverable costs of £2,178.45 i.e.

£800 + (20% of £5,000) + (15% of £2,523).

Additional costs for work in specified areas

25A.6   The areas referred to in rule 45.9(2) are (within London) the county court districts of Barnet, Bow, Brentford, Central London, Clerkenwell, Edmonton, Ilford, Lambeth, Mayors and City of London, Romford, Shoreditch, Wandsworth, West London, Willesden and Woolwich and (outside London) the county court districts of Bromley, Croydon, Dartford, Gravesend and Uxbridge.

Multiple claimants

25A.7   Where there is more than one potential claimant in relation to a dispute and two or more claimants instruct the same solicitor or firm of solicitors, the provisions of the section apply in respect of each claimant.

Information to be included in the claim form

25A.8   Costs only proceedings are commenced using the procedure set out in rule 44.12A. A claim form should be issued in accordance with Part 8. Where the claimant is claiming an amount of costs which exceed the amount of the fixed recoverable costs he must include on the claim form details of the exceptional circumstances which he considers justifies the additional costs.

25A.9   The claimant must also include on the claim form details of any disbursements or success fee he wishes to claim. The disbursements that may be claimed are set out in rule 45.10(1). If the disbursement falls within 45.10(2)(d) (disbursements that have arisen due to a particular feature of the dispute) the claimant must give details of the exceptional feature of the dispute and why he considers the disbursement to be necessary.

Disbursements and success fee

25A.10 If the parties agree the amount of the fixed recoverable costs and the only dispute is as to the payment of, or amount of, a disbursement or as to the amount of a success fee, then proceedings should be issued under rule 44.12A in the normal way and not by reference to Section II of Part 45.

See also Part 46, Court Service Forms

Author's note: This is the Direction as it exists but the reference to a dispute about a success fee (25A.10) has largely been overtaken by events as the success fee is now fixed (see Rule 45.11(2)), by virtue of the Civil Procedure (Amendment) (No 5) Rules 2003. (Statutory Instrument 2003 No. 3361 (L.38) as covered in the text.)

Disputes may still arise in relation to causes of action arising on or after 6th October 2003 where the solicitor entered into a conditional fee agreement on or before 29th February 2004.

APPENDIX C
SECTION 203
EMPLOYMENT RIGHTS ACT 1996

APPENDIX C
SECTION 203
EMPLOYMENT RIGHTS ACT 1996

203 – Restrictions on contracting out

(1)   Any provision in an agreement (whether a contract of employment or not) is void so far as it purports –

    (a) to exclude or limit the operation of any provision of this Act, or

    (b) to preclude a person from bringing any proceedings under this Act before an [employment tribunal].

(2)   Subsection (1) –

    (a) does not apply to any provision in a collective agreement excluding rights under section 28 if an order under section 35 is for the time being in force in respect of it,

    (b) does not apply to any provision in a dismissal procedures agreement excluding the right under section 94 if that provision is not to have effect unless an order under section 110 is for the time being in force in respect of it,

(c) does not apply to any provision in an agreement if an order under section 157 is for the time being in force in respect of it,

(d) ...

(e) does not apply to any agreement to refrain from instituting or continuing proceedings where a conciliation officer has taken action under section 18(1) of [the Employment Tribunals Act 1996], and

(f) does not apply to any agreement to refrain from instituting or continuing ...... any proceedings within [the following provisions of section 18(1) of the Employment Tribunals Act 1996 (cases where conciliation available) –

   (i) paragraph (d) (proceedings under this Act),

   (ii) paragraph (h) (proceedings arising out of the Part-time Workers (Prevention of Less Favourable Treatment) Regulations 2000,)]

   [(iii)] paragraph (i) (proceedings arising out of the Fixed-term Employees (Prevention of Less Favourable Treatment) Regulations 2002),

   (iv) paragraph (j) (proceedings under those Regulations),]

   if the conditions regulating compromise agreements under this Act are satisfied in relation to the agreement.

(3)   For the purposes of subsection (2)(f) the conditions regulating compromise agreements under this Act are that –

(a) the agreement must be in writing,

(b) the agreement must relate to the particular [proceedings],

(c) the employee or worker must have received [advice from a relevant independent adviser] as to the terms and effect of the proposed agreement and, in particular, its effect on his ability to pursue his rights before an [employment tribunal],

(d) there must be in force, when the adviser gives the advice, a [contract of insurance, or an indemnity provided for members of a professional body,] covering the risk of a claim by the employee or worker in respect of loss arising in consequence of the advice,

(e) the agreement must identify the adviser, and

(f) the agreement must state that the conditions regulating compromise agreements under this Act are satisfied.

[(3A)   A person is a relevant independent adviser for the purposes of subsection (3)(c) –

(a) if he is a qualified lawyer,

(b) if he is an officer, official, employee or member of an independent trade union who has been certified in writing by the trade union as competent to give advice and as authorised to do so on behalf of the trade union

(c) if he works at an advice centre (whether as an employee or a volunteer) and has been certified in writing by the centre as competent to give advice and as authorised to do so on behalf of the centre, or

(d) if he is a person of a description specified in an order made by the Secretary of State.

(3B)   But a person is not a relevant independent adviser for the purposes of subsection (3)(c) in relation to the employee or worker –

(a) if he is, is employed by or is acting in the matter for the employer or an associated employer,

(b) in the case of a person within subsection (3A)(b) or (c), if the trade union or advice centre is the employer or an associated employer,

(c) in the case of a person within subsection (3A)(c), if the employee or worker makes a payment for the advice received from him, or

(d) in the case of a person of a description specified in an order under subsection (3A)(d), if any condition specified in the order in relation to the giving of advice by persons of that description is not satisfied.

(4)   In subsection (3A)(a) "qualified lawyer" means –

(a) as respects England and Wales, a barrister (whether in practice as such or employed to give legal advice), a solicitor who holds a practising certificate, or a person other than a barrister or solicitor who is an authorised advocate or authorised litigator (within the meaning of the Courts and Legal Services Act 1990), and

(b) as respects Scotland, an advocate (whether in practice as such or employed to give legal advice), or a solicitor who holds a practising certificate.]

[(5)   An agreement under which the parties agree to submit a dispute to arbitration –

(a) shall be regarded for the purposes of subsection 2(e) and (f) as being an agreement to refrain from instituting or continuing proceedings if –

(i)   the dispute is covered by a scheme having effect by virtue of an order under section 212A of the Trade Union and Labour Relations (Consolidation Act 1992, and

(ii) the agreement is to submit it to arbitration in accordance with the scheme, but

(b) shall be regarded as neither being nor including such an agreement in any other case.]

APPENDIX D
PRECEDENT H OF THE SCHEDULE
OF COSTS PRECEDENTS

APPENDIX D
PRECEDENT H OF THE SCHEDULE
OF COSTS PRECEDENTS

SCHEDULE OF COSTS PRECEDENTS

PRECEDENT H

IN THE HIGH COURT OF JUSTICE   2000–B–9999

QUEEN'S BENCH DIVISION

BRIGHTON DISTRICT REGISTRY

BETWEEN

	AB	**Claimant**
	and	
	CD	**Defendant**

ESTIMATE OF CLAIMANT'S COSTS
DATED 12th APRIL 2001

The claimant instructed E F & Co under a conditional fee agreement dated 8th July 2000 in respect of which the following hourly rates are recoverable as base costs

Partner – £180 per hour plus VAT
Assistant Solicitor – £140 per hour plus VAT
Other fee earners – £85 per hour plus VAT

Item No.	Description of work done	V.A.T.	Disburse-ments	Profit Costs
	PART 1: **BASE COSTS ALREADY INCURRED**			
	8th July 2000 – EF & Co instructed			
	7th October 2000 – Claim issued			
1	Issue fee	—	£ 400.00	
	21st October 2000 – Particulars of claim served			
	25th November 2000 – Time for service of defence extended by agreement to 14th January 2001			
2	Fee on allocation	—	£ 80.00	
	20th January 2001 – case allocated to multi-track			
	9th February 2001 – Case management conference at which costs were awarded to the claimant and the base costs were summarily assessed at £400 (paid on 24th February 2001)			—
	23rd February 2001 – Claimant's list of documents			
	ATTENDANCES, COMMUNICATIONS AND WORK DONE			
	Claimant			
3	0.75 hours at £180			£ 135.00
4	4.4 hours at £140			£ 616.00
	To Summary	£ —	£ 480.00	£ 751.00

Item No.	Description of work done	V.A.T.	Disburse-ments	Profit Costs
5	**Witnesses of Fact** 3.8 hours at £140			£ 532.00
6	Paid travelling on 9th October 2000	£ 4.02	£ 22.96	
7	**Medical expert (Dr.IJ)** 1.5 hours at £140			£ 210.00
8	Dr. IJ''s fee for report		£ 350.00	
9	**Defendant and his solicitor** 2.5 hours at £140			£ 350.00
10	**Court (communications only)** 0.4 hours at £140			£ 56.00
11	**Documents** 0.75 hours at £180 and 22.25 hours at £140			£ 3,250.00
12	**Negotiations** 2.75 hours at £140			£ 385.00
13	VAT on solicitor's base fees	£ 968.45		
	To Summary	£ 972.47	£ 372.96	£ 4,783.00

Item No.	Description of work done	V.A.T.	Disburse-ments	Profit Costs
	PART 2: **BASE COSTS TO BE INCURRED**			
14	Fee on listing	—	£ 400.00	
15	Attendance at pre-trial review 5 hours at £140			£ 700.00
16	Counsel's base fee for pre-trial review		£ 750.00	
17	Attendance at trial 20 hours at £140			£ 2,800.00
18	Counsel's base fee for trial including refresher		£ 3,000.00	
19	Fee of expert witness (Dr. IJ)	—	£ 1,000.00	
20	Expenses of witnesses of fact	—	£ 150.00	
	ATTENDANCES, **COMMUNICATIONS AND** **WORK TO BE DONE**			
21	**Claimant** 1 hour at £180			£ 180.00
22	8 hours at £140			£ 1,120.00
23	**Witnesses of fact** 5 hours at £140			£ 700.00
24	**Medical expert (Dr. IJ)** 1 hour at £140			£ 140.00
25	**Defendant and his solicitor** 2 hours at £140			£ 280.00
	To Summary	£ —	£ 5,300.00	£ 5,920.00

Item No.	Description of work done	V.A.T.	Disburse-ments	Profit Costs
26	Court (communications only) 1 hour at £140			£ 140.00
27	Counsel (communications only) 3 hours at £140			£ 420.00
28	Documents 1 hour at £180, 25 hours at £140 and 15 hours at £85			£ 4,995.00
29	Negotiations 5 hours at £140			£ 700.00
30	Other work 5 hours at £140			£ 700.00
31	VAT on solicitor's base fees	£ 2,253.13		
	To Summary	£ 2,253.13	£ —	£ 6,955.00
	SUMMARY			
	Part 1			
	Page 1	£ —	£ 480.00	£ 751.00
	Page 2	£ 972.47	£ 372.96	£ 4,783.00
	Total base costs already incurred	£ 972.47	£ 852.96	£ 5,534.00
	Part 2			
	Page 2	£ —	£ 5,300.00	£ 5,920.00
	Page 3	£ 2,253.13	£ —	£ 6,955.00
	Total base costs already incurred	£ 2,253.13	£ 5,300.00	£12,875.00
	Total of base costs	£ 3,225.60	£ 6,152.96	£18,409.00
	Grand total			£27,787.56

APPENDIX E
COURT OF PROTECTION
PRACTICE NOTE: SOLICITORS
FIXED COSTS 9 DECEMBER 2003

APPENDIX E
COURT OF PROTECTION
PRACTICE NOTE: SOLICITORS
FIXED COSTS 9 DECEMBER 2003

It has been agreed with the Law Society that the amounts to be allowed will be as follows:

Category I

Work up to and including the date upon which the First General Order is entered – £665 (plus VAT). (The commencement fee, appointment fee, and fees for medical evidence and evidence of notification of the patient may be added. Please produce receipts for fees paid.)

Category II

(a) Preparation and lodgment of a receivership account – £175 (plus VAT)

(b) Preparation and lodgment of a receivership account which has been certified by a solicitor under the provisions of the Practice Notes dated 13 September 1984 and 5 March 1985 reported at [1984] 3 All ER 320 and [1985] 1 All ER 884 respectively – £190 (plus VAT).

Category III

General management work in the second and subsequent years

(a) where there are lay receivers and the Court has authorised the receiver to employ solicitors to carry out work not usually requiring professional assistance under rule 87 of the Court of Protection Rules 2001 – £175 (plus VAT)

(b) where there are professional receivers – £590 (plus VAT).

(Note: Categories II and III may be claimed together.)

Category IV

Applications under s.36(9) of the Trustee Act 1925 for the appointment of a new trustee in the place of the patient, for the purpose of making title to land – £320 (plus VAT).

Category V

In respect of conveyancing two elements will be allowable as follows:

(a) A sum of £125 in every case to cover correspondence with the Public Guardianship Office, the preparation of the certificate or affidavit of value and all other work solely attributable to the Court of Protection or the Public Guardianship Office, together with

(b) a value element of 0.5% of the consideration up to £400,000 and 0.25% thereafter, with a minimum sum for this element of £330.

As well as a fee for both the above elements, VAT and disbursements will be allowed.

New rates of fixed costs will apply as follows:–

in Category I, to all draft First General Orders sent out on or after I January 2004

in Category II, to all receivership accounts lodged on or after 1 January 2004

in Category III, to all general management costs in respect of years ended on or after 1 January 2004

in Category IV, to all orders sent out on or after 1 January 2004.

The amounts stated for each category are the maximum sum that may be claimed. If the value of the work is less than the maximum sum allowed, professionals may accept the lower amount without further reference to the Court.

In all categories, solicitors will continue to have the option of carrying out a detailed assessment of the costs rather than accepting fixed costs, if they wish. If solicitors seek an order for detailed assessment of the costs under Category II as well as Category III, the relevant items for both categories should be included in the same bill.

D.A. Lush, Master of the Court of Protection

9 December 2003

INDEX

Also by Kerry Underwood from emis professional publishing

NEW!

Practice Management and Funding

This new service builds on Kerry Underwood's authoritative position as a leading thinker on funding and costs issues for litigators. His original perspectives will be shared in this new quarterly newsletter which focuses on how practices should change to survive in the changing funding environment.

- Litigation Funding
- Cash flow
- Work flow
- Technology
- Outsourcing

- Taxation
- Contentious and non-contentious costs
- Conditional and contingency fees
- Fixed costs developments

No Win No Fee, Fixed Costs and many years of lecturing mean that thousands of lawyers already know that Kerry's views are rooted in the way that solicitors' practices work. His concerns are the concerns of all partners and managers trying to combine delivery of justice with building a profitable practice.

For a Free Sample ring 0870 122 5525 or fax 0113 380 3423

Employment Law and Litigation

This monthly service is full of material not just to update, but to build your practice and to increase its efficiency. Coverage is comprehensive – and in 2004 enhanced by an email alerter so that you will receive an update every 2 weeks:

- Contracts and contract terms
- Redundancies
- Sex, race and disability discrimination
- Tribunal practice and procedure
- County court litigation

- Skills and tactics
- Funding issues
- European law
- US developments which often foreshadow our own.

Its clear format is ideal for rapid absorption of information. The Editorial Team Includes: Kerry Underwood and Marc Jones from Underwoods, Dominic Regan and Mark Hodgson, a solicitor practising in industry.

For a Free Sample ring 0870 122 5525 or fax 0113 380 3423

Other Recent PI Titles from xpl law

Tripping and Slipping

Denis Carey, Solicitor, Crichtons Solicitors

Tripping and slipping cases are a high percentage of PI practitioners' work. But they have a relatively low value per case. So, all lawyers in this area need an easily accessible and practical summary to help in risk assessment process and during the action. Focusing on key day to day practice issues, lawyers (of whatever experience) are provided with a perfect checklist to progress a case without hitches or wasted time.

Contents:

- Introduction and Case Preparation
- Highways
- Premises
- Slips & Trips at work

ISBN 1 85811 285 0   £28.00

Work Related Injury Litigation: A Practitioner's Handbook

Tim Meakin, Three Serjeants Inn and Dr Peter Ellis, Lamb Chambers, Barristers

Clear and accessible, this book provides personal injury and clinical negligence practitioners with the only up to date single volume paperback covering this increasingly crucial area of work. Each chapter includes sections on practice and procedure, medical background and expert evidence and quantifying the claim as appropriate covering:

- The legal framework: causation, the duty of care and limitation
- Deafness and tinnitus
- Occupational cancers
- Occupational asthma, asbestosis and other respiratory diseases
- Vibration induced disorders
- Occupational infections and skin diseases
- Work related upper limb and spinal disorders
- Stress at work
- Specimen Particulars of Claim, Defences, Schedules of loss and damage

£44.00   ISBN: 1 85811 315 6   September 2003

---

xpl ... law explained.
To Order Ring 01494 772973 or Fax 01494 793951

Printed in the United Kingdom
by Lightning Source UK Ltd.
100614UKS00002B/1-60

9 781858 113234